WEBB SOCIETY DEEP-SKY OBSERVER'S HANDBOOK

VOLUME 7
THE SOUTHERN SKY

WEBB SOCIETY DEEP-SKY OBSERVER'S HANDBOOK

VOLUME 7
THE SOUTHERN SKY

Compiled by the Webb Society
    Edited by Kenneth Glyn Jones, F.R.A.S.
    Written and illustrated by Steven J. Hynes.

With a foreword by Professor Gerard de Vaucouleurs
(McDonald Observatory, University of Texas)

ENSLOW PUBLISHERS, INC.

Bloy St. & Ramsey Ave.	P.O. Box 38
Box 777	Aldershot
Hillside, N.J. 07205	Hants GU12 6BP
U.S.A.	U.K.

Library of Congress Cataloging in Publication Data
(Revised for vol. 6-7)

Webb Society deep-sky observer's handbook.

First published under title: The Webb Society
observers handbook, 1975-   .
Vols. 6-   : published by Enslow Publishers,
Hillside, N.J.
Includes bibliographies.
Contents: v. 1. Double stars – v. 2. Planetary
and gaseous nebulae – v. 3. Open and globular
clusters – v. 4. Galaxies – v. 5. Clusters of
galaxies – v. 6. Anonymous galaxies – v. 7.
The Southern sky.
1. Astronomy—Observers' manuals. I. Jones,
Kenneth Glyn. II. Webb Society. III. Title.
QB64.W36 1979   523.8'9   78-31260
ISBN 0-89490-027-7 (v. 1)

Printed in the United States of America

10 9 8 7 6 5 4 3

To Professor G. de Vaucouleurs,
World-ranging astronomer,
With admiration and gratitude.

CONTENTS

List of illustrations   viii
Foreword   ix
General Preface to the Handbook series   xiii
Editor's Preface to Volume 7: The Southern Sky   xv

PART ONE: HISTORICAL REVIEW
Introduction   1
Early Explorations   1
Halley at St. Helena   2
Lacaille at the Cape   2
The 'Gentlemen Scientists'   4
Harvard and Lick in South America   8
Twentieth Century Astronomy in South Africa   9
Modern Southern Observatories   11
The Anglo-Australian Telescope   12
The Future   13

PART TWO: EXTENDED DESCRIPTIONS OF SELECTED OBJECTS
NGC   55: SCULPTOR   15
NGC   253: SCULPTOR   15
Small Magellanic Cloud   16
Fornax Cluster of Galaxies   17
Large Magellanic Cloud   19
NGC 3372 and η Carinae   20
NGC 5128: CENTAURUS   21
NGC 5139 (ω CENTAURI)   22
NGC 5236 (M.83): HYDRA   23
NGC 6514 (M.20): SAGITTARIUS   24
NGC 6523/30 (M.8): SAGITTARIUS   24
NGC 7293: AQUARIUS   25

PART THREE: CATALOGUE OF OBSERVATIONS
Introduction & Observers   27
Section 1: Open Clusters   30
Section 2: Globular Clusters   58
Section 3: Planetary Nebulae   79
Section 4: Diffuse Nebulae   97
Section 5: Galaxies   109
Section 6: The Magellanic Clouds   141

CONTENTS

PART FOUR: APPENDICES
1. Travelling with a Telescope   159
2. Observing the Large Magellanic Cloud   162
3. Observing the Small Magellanic Cloud   171
4. W.S.Q.J. Articles Relating to Southern Sky Objects   173
5. Observational Data Relating to the Star η Carinae   176
6. The Gum Nebula and Related Features   179
7. Catalogue of Additional Objects   187

BIBLIOGRAPHY   195

LIST OF ILLUSTRATIONS

Fornax Cluster of Galaxies   18
Reference Contour Chart of the LMC   164
Detailed Charts of Selected Areas of the LMC   165 – 170
Reference Chart of the SMC   172
1° Field Chart of η Carinae   176
Light-curve of η Carinae   178

Catalogue Illustrations
Field Drawings of Open Clusters   49 – 57
Field Drawings of Globular Clusters   74 – 78
Field Drawings of Planetary Nebulae   91 – 96
Field Drawings of Diffuse Nebulae   105 – 108
Field Drawings of Galaxies   135 – 140
Field Drawings of the Magellanic Clouds   148 – 157

FOREWORD

    The southern skies hold a special attraction for astronomers, a unique fascination for deep-sky observers. Even today when air travel and space flights have shrunken the world and dulled our sense of wonder, only a small minority of amateur (and indeed professional) astronomers have had the glorious experience of 'discovering' for themselves the southern heavens in all their multifarious splendour. To view and study that part of the Universe which does not rise above the horizons of the populous centres of the northern hemisphere is indeed an unforgettable experience and precious opportunity.

    I remember vividly the sense of awe and keen anticipation when I began my exploration of the Magellanic Clouds and of the brighter southern galaxies at Mount Stromlo Observatory in 1951 as the first Research Fellow in the newly created Department of Astronomy of the Australian National University. It is not just that the scarcity of astronomers and observatories south of the equator made almost any new observation worth making, because so much remained (and still remains) to be done in the southern sky. What makes it so attractive is, above all, the overwhelming abundance of unusual, outstanding or beautiful stars, nebulae and galaxies and the unique advantages of a southern location to study some of the most important astronomical objects: the Milky Way and its countless nebulae and star clusters, the Magellanic Clouds, and the world of galaxies beyond.

    Just think of the riches that Nature has accumulated south of, say, $-30°$ declination, in just one quarter of the celestial sphere: the centre of our Galaxy, only dimly seen through the haze near the southern horizon from most northern climes, can only be appreciated in its incredible brilliancy when it culminates overhead at midnight in the dark, freezing nights of the southern winter. Likewise, the beauty and extent of the 'Gould Belt' of bright blue hot stars, inclined some 16 degrees to the main galactic plane, can be really appreciated only from southern latitudes. Stretching from Carina to Scorpius and beyond its stars, reinforcing the light from the central sector of the Milky Way, can produce a visible illumination of terrestrial clouds at night.

    Next, think of the 'Coal Sack', the most prominent of the great clouds of interstellar dust, and just in front of it the striking (if somewhat over-advertised) 'Southern Cross' - the symbol par excellence of the southern skies which Australia and Brazil have emblazoned on their national flags. Any small telescope will show in it the sparkling star cluster, κ Crucis, the famous 'Jewel Box' of John Herschel, possibly the most beautiful of all galactic (open) clusters. Close by the Cross we see the nearest and brightest double star, α Centauri, of which each

x

component is a good replica of our Sun, and its fainter proper motion
companion 'Proxima Centauri', the nearest of all the stars. Not only do
the southern heavens harbour the nearest as well as the brightest stars
visible to the naked eye, Sirius and Canopus, but they offer some of the
rarest types of stars, such as η Carinae, the star which briefly rivalled
Sirius in 1843 only to fade to relative obscurity – but not
insignificance – some decades later, although it had brightened again to
about 7th magnitude when I first saw it in 1952 during my 'getting
acquainted' tour of the southern constellations (1). As a grandiose
background for this mysterious object Nature has placed one of the
brightest, most complex and spectacular emission nebulosities of the whole
sky, the great 'η Carinae Nebula', criss-crossed by obscuring dust lanes
and some dark clouds, of which the most prominent is the famous 'Keyhole',
as John Herschel called it because of its contorted shape. Not far from
it the photometrists will find two of the brightest, hottest blue stars in
the sky: ζ Puppis and γ Velorum. The whole area is pervaded by the giant
'Gum Nebula', possibly the largest H II ring nebulosity in the whole sky,
produced long ago by a supernova whose remnant (Vela X) is near its
centre; it can be photographed (through a narrow band Hα filter) with
the smallest cameras.

It is also in the southern sky that we find the two brightest globular
star clusters, ω Centauri and 47 Tucanae, both easily visible to the
naked eye as 4th magnitude nebulous 'stars' (the brightest in the
northern hemisphere, the famous M.13 cluster in Hercules is only a poor
third). Both offer striking spectacles even in modest telescopes and the
views through large instruments are simply stupendous.

But all this pales into insignificance compared with the unique,
grandiose view of the Magellanic Clouds, the two galaxies nearest to our
Milky Way Galaxy, which John Herschel described as 'systems sui generis
and without analogue in our (northern) hemisphere'. Because of their
proximity – a mere 150,000 light-years for the Large Cloud, less than
one fifteenth of the distance of the Andromeda Galaxy – a modest camera
will record more detail in the Clouds than large observatory telescopes

---

1. A search of the patrol plate collection at Riverview College Observatory
by Fr. D.J.K. O'Connell later revealed that the star had actually
brightened in 1941, and no one had noticed it for more than 10 years!
A striking illustration of the wide gaps in our patrol of the southern
sky (for the story of η Carinae see Leaflet No. 281 of the Astronomical
Society of the Pacific, 1952; see also the light-curve and finding
chart in Appendix 5).

record in most other galaxies (2). Visually, the best instruments to
view the Magellanic Clouds and the great star clouds and dark nebulae
along the path of the southern Milky Way are wide-field binoculars (the
visible size of the Large Cloud is 8 degrees, of the Small Cloud, 3
degrees (3)). A war surplus 80-mm German AA binocular with sturdy tripod
and headrest that I had brought to Mount Stromlo gave me breathtaking
views of the Clouds and southern Milky Way; showing stars to the 11th
magnitude in a 6 degree field it was almost like viewing the famous
Barnard photographic atlas. Such an instrument would also make an
excellent comet-seeker with a better chance of original discovery than in
the more exploited northern sky.

Beyond the Clouds, it is also in the southern hemisphere that we find
the brightest, largest and nearest galaxies outside the Local Group:
objects such as NGC 55, 247, 253, 300 and 7793 in the Sculptor Group - a
ring-like structure 20 degrees in apparent diameter - at distances of 2 to
3 megaparsecs from us, each subtends 10 to 20 arc-minutes and can be seen,
or better, photographed, with very modest telescopes and cameras, and can
be spotted with binoculars. Other spectacular galaxies are NGC 5128 - the
Centaurus A radio source - a probable collision between a giant elliptical
and an uncautious spiral which ventured too close and was trapped in the
powerful gravitational field of the monster galaxy. Its characteristic
broad, dark lane, hiding the centre of the elliptical component, can be
easily seen with small telescopes and can be clearly photographed with a
5-inch, f/5 camera such as the WW I Zeiss camera I used at Mount Stromlo
to compare it to more distant galaxies suspected to be of similar type,
such as NGC 1316 - the Fornax A radio source - and NGC 1947 - one of the
original 'dusty ellipticals' - photographed with the 30-inch Reynolds
reflector. The southern sky is full of large and, to this day, still
little-known galaxies, such as NGC 1313 - an interacting pair of an SB(s)d
spiral with a magellanic spiral or irregular; NGC 1291 - the prototype of
a late barred lenticular (or SB0) galaxy with a magnificent outer ring
(it looks like a halation ring on the old Franklin-Adams charts); NGC 1365
and NGC 2442-3, two beautiful, typical barred spirals, the latter in
interaction with an elliptical companion, NGC 2434. One should mention

---

2. As a matter of fact, in order to study the spiral structure of the
Clouds I had first to find a 'telescope' small enough to show them as
galaxies that could be compared with others recorded using large
reflectors. I finally settled for a standard 35-mm camera with 50 -,
35-, and even 28-mm focus lenses, and - for really detailed study - on
a twin camera equipped with WW II Aero-Ektar 7-inch (178 mm) focus
lenses which give superb definition over a 20° field when stopped to
f/4, recording stars down to mag. 14.3(pg) in a 1 hour exposure on
Kodak 103a-O emulsion. I counted over 150,000 stars on just 3 such
plates (2 covering the LMC, 1 covering the SMC) (Astronomical Journal,
60, 126, 219, 1955).
3. On a drawing of the Large Cloud by John Herschel with the modest
binoculars of his time, the typical asymmetric barred spiral structure
of the SBm type can be seen (see IAU Symp. 58, Canberra, 1973, p.1).

also NGC 1433, the prototype of the barred, ringed galaxies, SB(r), recently analyzed in great detail by Ronald J. Buta, whose visual observations of many southern galaxies with the telescopes at Siding Spring Observatory grace this volume; NGC 5236 (M.83), the prototype of the transition between ordinary and barred spirals of the S-shaped variety (SAB(s)), is observable with some difficulty from northern observatories, but it is really a magnificent object when seen overhead; NGC 6744, the largest example of a multi-armed spiral at the transition stage between ordinary and barred systems, SAB(r) (4). One cannot discuss galaxies, however, without mentioning supernovae and the magnificent work done in recent years by the Rev. Robert Evans of Australia, who has set new records in the visual search and discovery of these rare and stupendous stellar explosions. While supernovae do not occur more often in the southern sky, the number of active hunters is much smaller than in the northern hemisphere, and the more widespread distribution of galaxies makes it an all year sport, while the search in the northern sky is too often unduly concentrated in the Virgo Cluster and the supergalactic plane where the galaxies congregate, making it more a springtime activity. All it takes is a small telescope – anything in the 6- to 10-inch (15 – 30 cm.) range will do –, a thorough knowledge of where the galaxies are and what they normally look like, keen eyes and a lot of patience. The importance to modern astronomy of an early discovery and announcement of supernovae cannot be exaggerated, and the fact of the matter is that in spite of repeated, and prodigiously expensive efforts by professionals to devise automated methods of searching for them, most have been (and still are) discovered visually by amateurs with small telescopes or cameras, and a good knowledge of deep-sky wonders.

The present volume with its many illustrations of visual observations of the more striking celestial curiosities of the southern sky with instruments ranging from the smallest binoculars to the 3.9 m. Anglo-Australian Telescope is a useful addition to the very short list of specialised earlier works on this subject (5). It should be an inspiring guide to its readers. I am grateful to its Editor for giving me this opportunity to reminisce about my own unforgettable memories of this most fascinating part of the heavens.

Gerard de Vaucouleurs
McDonald Observatory, Univ. of Texas.

---

4. I could go on forever discussing my favourite topic. The interested reader will find an illustrated guide to the southern Shapley-Ames galaxies (south of Dec. -35°) in 'Sky & Telescope', 16, 520, 582, 1957 and in 'Memoirs of the Commonwealth Observatory', Vol. III, No. 13 Canberra, 1956. For a history of the early studies of southern galaxies, see Occasional Notes of the R.A.S., No. 16, 1956.

5. E.J. Hartung's 'Astronomical Objects for Southern Telescopes', Cambridge University Press, 1968, and, for the French reader, J. Sagot and J. Texereau, 'Revue des Constellations', including a fine atlas of charts, published by Societe Astronomique de France (1st edition, 1963, 2nd edition, 1985).

GENERAL PREFACE

Named after the Rev. T.W. Webb (1807 - 1885), an eminent amateur
astronomer and author of the classic <u>Celestial Objects for Common
Telescopes</u>, the Webb Society exists to encourage the study of double stars
and other deep-sky objects. It has members in almost every country where
amateur astronomy flourishes. It has a number of Observing Sections,
organised by an experienced director; these include Double Stars, Nebulae
and Clusters, Galaxies and Southern Sky. Publications include a Quarterly
Journal, containing articles, special features, book reviews and section
reports. Membership is open to anyone whose interests are compatible;
enquiries and membership forms are available from the Secretary, Steven J.
Hynes, 8 Cormorant Close, Sydney, Crewe, Cheshire CW1 1LN, England, or
the North America Secretary, Ronald J. Morales, 1440 South Marmora, Tucson,
Arizona 85713, U.S.A.

Webb's <u>Celestial Objects for Common Telescopes</u>, first published in 1859,
must have been amongst the most popular books of its kind ever written.
Running through six editions by 1917, it is still in print, although the
text is of more historical than practical interest to the amateur of today.
Not only has knowledge of the Universe been transformed by modern
developments, but the present generation of amateur astronomers has
telescopes and other equipment that even the professional of Webb's day
would have envied.

The aim of the <u>Webb Society Deep-Sky Observer's Handbook</u> is to provide
a series of observers manuals that do justice to the equipment that is
available today and to cover fields that have not been adequately covered
by other organisations of amateurs. We have tried to make these guides
the best of their kind; they are written by experts, some of them
professional astronomers, who have had considerable practical experience
with the pleasures and problems of the amateur astronomer. The manuals
can be used profitably by the beginner, who will find much to stimulate
enthusiasm and imagination. However, they are designed primarily for the
more experienced amateur who seeks greater scope for the exercise of his
skills.

Each Handbook is complete with regard to its subject. The reader is
given an adequate historical and theoretical basis for a modern
understanding of the physical role of the objects covered in the wider
context of the Universe. He is provided with a thorough exposition of
observing methods, including the construction and operation of ancillary
equipment such as micrometers and simple spectroscopes. Each volume
contains a detailed and comprehensive catalogue of objects for the
amateur to locate and to observe with an eye made more perceptive by the

knowledge he has gained. We hope that these volumes will enable the reader to extend his abilities, to exploit his telescope to its limits, and to tackle the challenging difficulties of new fields of observation with confidence of success.

EDITOR'S PREFACE
VOLUME 7: THE SOUTHERN SKY

Previous volumes in this series have been confined to areas of the sky north of about 20° south declination. The only reason for this is that our membership at that time was almost entirely confined to observers living north of the equator. In recent years, however, not only have more observers in Australia, New Zealand and Africa joined our ranks, but many more 'northerners' have travelled extensively to regions where the splendours of the southern sky may be explored.

The happy results of this activity are demonstrated in this volume, which although far from exhaustive of southern treasures, nevertheless provides a more than adequate guide to most of the glittering prizes to be attained there. Naturally, some degree of overlap with the contents of previous volumes has been inevitable, but the main effort has been devoted to objects of lower southerly declination.

The book opens, in Part One, with a concise but thorough historical review of optical astronomy in the southern hemisphere, ranging from Edmond Halley's 1676-7 expedition to St. Helena, the Abbe Lacaille's visit to the Cape of Good Hope in 1751, and the establishment of many other observatories in South Africa, South America and Australia to the present day.

In Part Two, detailed guides are provided for selected objects such as the Large and Small Magellanic Clouds, the region of η Carinae, the Fornax Cluster of galaxies, and a number of other splendid objects in the bright starfields of Sagittarius and Scorpius.

The main Catalogue, in Part 3, describes, with numerous illustrations, some 300 objects of all classes in six sections, the observations having been made by Webb Society members in many parts of the world and using instruments ranging from 12x40 binoculars to a 158-inch (4 meter) reflector.

This up-to-date compilation, while acknowledging the value of previous publications such as those of Sagot and Texereau, and the late E.J. Hartung, should prove a valuable observing guide for southern astronomers and an indispensable pocket book for the 'travelling' astronomers of both hemispheres.

The writing of the book, the collation of observations and the execution of the illustrations have been carried out with assiduous care by the Webb Society's Secretary, Steven J. Hynes, who, as a British civil servant, and resident in a latitude of 53° North, is an unrepentant northerner. Even so, he has travelled and observed extensively to such south-accessible regions as Sri Lanka, Tenerife and Crete. With a $4\frac{1}{4}$-inch RFT wrapped up in a beach-towel in a hold-all and a star atlas at the bottom of his suitcase, he can claim to be the model of the well-equipped 'touring astronomer'. He has been a devoted deep-sky observer for many years: he gained the coveted Webb Society Award in 1973 for his outstanding articles on Ursa Major Galaxies and Globular Clusters, and since 1981 has ably filled the dual role of Secretary to the Society and 'producer' of our Quarterly Journal. The Editor, and the Society, owe Steve and all those loyal members who have contributed observations to this volume, an immense debt of gratitude for their devoted efforts.

Finally, our most sincere thanks is due to Professor de Vaucouleurs for granting us the honour of accepting the dedication of this volume, and for generously providing a Foreword which must whet the appetite of any itinerant astronomer. We are grateful also for his invaluable advice and for allowing us to use his own light-curve for η Carinae.

Professor de Vaucouleurs is an astronomer of international eminence whose researches have led him to explore the southern skies as widely as those of the northern hemisphere. In addition, his interest in, and encouragement of, the activities of amateur astronomers have long endeared him to their community: for this, we can all be grateful.

Author's Acknowledgements

Work on this volume has been aided on three levels. Firstly, by the efforts of the contributors; in this respect I would very much like to thank David A. Allen, Ronald J. Buta, Denis Dutton, Colin Henshaw, Victor Hirsch, Ronald J. Morales and Malcolm J. Thomson for their significant help, but particularly Jeffrey A. Corder who submitted a substantial volume of material and assisted by his enthusiasm for the project.

Secondly, the practical task of compiling the volume was greatly aided by the advice and experience of Kenneth Glyn Jones F.R.A.S. and Edmund S. Barker F.R.A.S. The role of Professor Gerard de Vaucouleurs should also be recognised; his excellent Foreword and enthusiastic response are much appreciated.

Finally, on the 'home front', my task was eased by the patience of my wife Julie who took much of the burden of our baby daughter Carina while I was busy working on drawings or at the typewriter.

Steven J. Hynes

PART ONE

HISTORICAL REVIEW

Historical Review

Introduction

For many thousands of years Man has observed the skies and noted the changes, the waxing and waning of the Moon, the movements of the planets and the changes of the star patterns visible with the seasons. Almost every culture has incorporated these observations into its myths and religious and agricultural lore.

In China, Japan and Korea, particularly detailed observational records were made for astrological purposes from quite an early time in history (c. 4000 B.C.). These have proved invaluable to modern researchers studying comets, novae and supernovae. However, the more scientific collection of data and investigation of celestial phenomena did not arise until a few centuries B.C., and then in the Mediterranean and Middle East cultures. With the passage of centuries and the rise and collapse of civilizations, modern astronomy, together with so much other science and art, was born in the flowering of European culture during the Renaissance, around the 15th century A.D.

Early Explorations

As a result of the Renaissance, European explorers ventured further than ever before, resulting in their discovery of the Americas and the opening of trade links with the mysterious lands of the Far East. As they sailed southwards the familiar star patterns, so essential to navigation, slipped below the horizon to be replaced by new sights including a particularly curious phenomenon, two patches of light, like the Milky Way, but separated by some distance from that great, broad arch that spans the sky.

The 'Cape Clouds', as they were called by the 15th and 16th century sailors, were found to be of navigational importance. The southern sky has no conspicuous 'Polaris', but the Clouds and the South Celestial Pole form a rough equilateral triangle, enabling the position of the South Celestial Pole to be identified and an approximate latitude determined. One early observer of the Clouds described them thus: ".... two clouds of reasonable bigness moving about the place of the pole continually now rising and now falling, so keeping their continual course in circular moving". The Clouds received the appellation 'Magellanic' following their description by Pigafetta and in honour of Ferdinand Magellan's circumnavigation of the world in 1518 - 1521. Strictly, Magellan did not complete the circumnavigation, as he was killed at Cebo on 1521 April 27 but is generally (and rightly) credited with completing the 'missing' section. The tiny, battered, Portuguese fleet, now under the command of

Historical Review

Sebastian el Cano, did not reach Seville until the August of 1522.

Halley at St. Helena

The first specifically astronomical expedition to the southern
hemisphere was that of Edmond Halley. The son of a wealthy and influential
London merchant, he showed great promise from quite an early age. Even as
an undergraduate at Queen's College, Oxford, he developed an improved
method of determining the elements of planetary orbits. He also found
that tables of star positions available were in drastic need of revision
and were vital to the advancement of astronomy and navigation. Flamsteed
had begun to catalogue the stars of the northern sky, and Halley, at the
age of just 20, took it upon himself to catalogue the southern sky. He
used his influence with the East India Company to obtain free passage to
the tiny island of St. Helena (latitude 17° South) in the South Atlantic
where he spent almost 2 years during 1676 - 1677 accurately cataloguing
the positions of some 360 stars, and in the process, discovering the non-
stellar nature of omega Centauri. He also observed the well-known cluster
M.7 (NGC 6475) and was an independent discoverer of the cluster NGC 6231.
The latter had been found by Hodierna, observing from Sicily, in 1654. In
addition, Halley observed a transit of Mercury across the Sun. By the age
of 23, with the publication of his 'Catalogus Stellarum Australium' in
1679, his reputation was made. Flamsteed referred to him as the 'Southern
Tycho' and, although he had left Oxford in 1676 without taking his degree,
he was granted his M.A. by Royal Mandate and subsequently elected F.R.S.

In later years, of course, Halley made other great contributions to
astronomy, particularly in his study of comets and prediction of the
periodic nature of the comet which now bears his name. Also, his careful
observations of Sirius, Procyon and Arcturus in 1718 brought about his
discovery of the proper motion of these stars.

Lacaille at the Cape

Despite Halley's expedition it must be said that probably the most
significant exploration of the southern heavens prior to the nineteenth
century was that of Abbé Nicholas-Louis de la Caille, who spent two years
at the Cape of Good Hope, in South Africa, from 1751 April 19 to 1753
March 8. This most productive trip resulted in positions being determined
for 9776 southern stars and a catalogue of 42 nebulae and clusters (see
Table 1). The star catalogue was not published until 1763, the year after
his death, but his observations of the nebulae and clusters appeared in a
Mémoire of the Académie Royale des Sciences, in 1755. From his

Historical Review

observations, Lacaille was able to classify these objects into three
types or 'species':

> I   - nebulae without stars
> II   - clusters of stars
> III - stars with nebulosity.

Fourteen objects of each type were found, though some are not now
identifiable. His descriptions were usually quite limited so do not
provide many clues which would help in tracking them down. Position
errors could account for the discrepancies, or perhaps one or two were
unrecognised comets.

. . . . -

Table 1. Lacaille's Catalogue of Southern Nebulae and Clusters.

	Type 1	Type II	Type III
1.	NGC 104 (GCl.)	?	?
2.	NGC 2070 (neb.)	Asterism	NGC 2547 (OCl.)
3.	NGC 2477 (OCl.)	NGC 2516 (OCl.)	?
4.	NGC 4833 (GCl.)	NGC 2546 (OCl.)	IC 2488 (OCl.)
5.	NGC 5139 (GCl.)	IC 2391 (OCl.)	NGC 3372 (neb.)
6.	NGC 5236 (Gal.)	?	
7.	NGC 5281 (OCl.)	NGC 3228 (OCl.)	NGC 3766 (OCl.)
8.	NGC 6124 (OCl.)	?	NGC 5662 (OCl.)
9.	NGC 6121 (GCl.)	IC 2602 (OCl.)	Asterism
10.	NGC 6242 (OCl.)	NGC 3532 (OCl.)	NGC 6025 (OCl.)
11.	NGC 6637 (GCl.)	Asterism	NGC 6397 (GCl.)
12.	NGC 6656 (GCl.)	NGC 4755 (OCl.)	NGC 6405 (OCl.)
13.	?	NGC 6231 (OCl.)	NGC 6523/30 (Neb. & OCl.)
14.	NGC 6809 (GCl.)	NGC 6475 (OCl.)	?

. . . .

Of the true nebulae and clusters in Lacaille's list, he was the first
observer of 23, adding considerably to the total of 36 known in both
hemispheres up to that time.

Lacaille seems to have adopted the Galilean view of the nature of
nebulae, that is, that they could ultimately be resolved into stars: "I
will not venture further than to speculate that the nebulae of the first
species are no more than small portions of the Milky Way, spread

throughout different regions of the sky and that the nebulae of the third species are only stars which are found, relative to us, in a straight line as we observe these luminous patches" (ref. 1).

Whilst at the Cape, Lacaille also observed the Magellanic Clouds: "In frequent examination with a 14-foot telescope of the areas of the Milky Way where its whiteness is most noticeable, and comparing them with the two clouds, commonly called the Magellanic Clouds ..... it is obvious that the white portions of the sky resemble one another so perfectly that one believes, without too much conjecture, that they are of the same nature, or, if you like, that these clouds are no more than detached portions of the Milky Way which are themselves composed merely of parts often interrupted" (ref. 1). He also commented on the 'Coalsack', the large dark nebula in Crux: "a space of almost 3 degrees extent in all directions which appears as a dense blackness in the eastern part of the Southern Cross".

It is also to Lacaille, incidentally, that we owe the names of many of the smaller southern constellations. Antlia (the air-pump), Caelum (the chisel), Circinus (the compasses), Fornax (the furnace), Horologium (the clock), Mensa (named after Table Mountain, Cape of Good Hope), Microscopium (the microscope), Norma (the square), Octans (the octant), Pictor (the painter's easel), Pyxis (the compass), Reticulum (the net), Sculptor (the sculptor) and Telescopium (the telescope) were all created by Lacaille.

The 'Gentleman Scientists'

The progress of astronomy in the southern hemisphere really started to accelerate in the early nineteenth century, particularly in South Africa and Australia as settlement and development of the new lands began. Perhaps the first permanent observatory of any significance was that set up in the 1820's by the British Admiralty at the Cape of Good Hope. The first director of this observatory was Fearon Fallows, who arrived at the Cape in June 1821 with a small Dollond transit telescope and an altazimuth refractor by Ramsden. On landing, he began to prepare the plans for the future permanent observatory and also started to measure the positions of the brighter stars visible from that location. The resulting catalogue of 273 stars was presented to the Royal Society on 1824 February 26. Working from a tent as a temporary measure, construction of the permanent installations began in the December of 1826 and new instruments were fixed in place during early 1829, enabling work to begin in earnest. Unfortunately, Fallows' observations were seriously disrupted in 1830 by health problems as first he caught scarlatina and then dropsy. In early

Historical Review

1831 this got so bad that each day he had to be carried in a blanket from
his sick-room to the observatory. His problems were made worse by the
departure of his only assistant, Captain Ronald, in October 1830, and he
would have been forced to discontinue his work altogether if his wife had
not by this time qualified herself to act as his assistant. Even so, by
April 1831 he was no longer able to work, and died on 1831 July 25.

Fallows was replaced by Thomas Henderson, who arrived at the Cape in
April, 1832. Though he remained there for only thirteen months before
resigning because of poor health, his achievements were not inconsiderable.
He made over 5000 observations of the places of southern stars, but his
most important achievement was the measurement of the parallax of
α Centauri, which he estimated to be about 1" (now refined to 0".75).
This was announced to the Royal Astronomical Society on 1839 January 2,
almost simultaneously with the announcements of Bessel and Struve on their
parallaxes of 61 Cygni and Vega. The importance of these discoveries is
reflected in the words of Sir John Herschel at the presentation of the
gold medal of the R.A.S. to Bessel for his discovery: "Gentlemen of the
Royal Astronomical Society - I congratulate you and myself that we have
lived to see the great and hitherto impassable barrier to our excursion
into the sidereal universe, that barrier against which we have chafed so
long and so vainly ...... almost simultaneously overleaped at three
different points. It is the greatest and most glorious triumph which
practical astronomy has ever witnessed" (ref. 2).

The third Royal Astronomer at the Cape of Good Hope, Sir Thomas
Maclear, was originally a surgeon and became interested in astronomy
through an acquaintance with Admiral W.H. Smyth, whom he met after having
taken on the post of house surgeon at Bedford Infirmary in 1815. He
proved himself to be an avid observer and mathematician and by 1830 had
built a transit telescope as part of a small observatory at his home in
Biggleswade. He took up his post as astronomer at the Cape in 1833,
actually arriving in Cape Town in January 1834, just ten days before Sir
John Herschel.

Maclear made a large number of observations of star positions and
double star measures, to the extent that many of his early measurements
had to be left unreduced. He supervised the installation of a 7-inch
(17.8 cm.) Merz refractor in 1850 and a transit circle, identical to the
one at Greenwich, in 1855. As well as recording star positions, he also
observed the spectacular increase in brightness of η Carinae from 1837 to
its maximum in 1843.

The main contribution to knowledge of the southern skies at this time

Historical Review

though, was undoubtedly made by Sir John Herschel, the brilliant and precocious son of Sir William Herschel. Having defied his father's wishes that he should join the clergy, he left home in January 1814 to study law. After eighteen months he became disenchanted and took up teaching at St. John's, Cambridge, but decided this life was not for him either: "I am grown full, fat and stupid. Pupillizing has done this - and I have not made one of my cubs understand what I would have them drive at" (ref. 3). 1816 brought about a reconciliation with his father and he wrote to his friend Charles Babbage (the inventor of the remarkable 'differential engine' which led to other mechanical - and later, electronic - computers) that he had agreed to take up ".... under my father's directions .... the series of his observations where he has left them and continuing his scrutiny of the heavens with powerful telescopes" (ref. 3).

After the death of his father he pursued his interests in numerous directions, particularly astronomy, optics and chemistry, until, on 1833 November 13, he set sail from Portsmouth on the 'Mountstuart Elphinstone' with his wife, three children and numerous items of astronomical equipment, heading for South Africa.

Landing at Cape Town on 16th January 1834, the Herschel family set up home at Feldhausen, about six miles (10 km.) from Cape Town. Little time was wasted setting up the equipment, an 18¾-inch (48 cm.) speculum reflector of 20-foot (6.1 m.) focal length and a 7-inch (17.8 cm.) refractor, enabling the first observation, of α Crucis, to be made on February 22.

Sir John Herschel remained at the Cape until 1838, making extensive observations of nebulae, clusters and double stars, which were published on his return as 'Results of Astronomical Observations made during the Years 1834, 5, 6, 7, 8, at the Cape of Good Hope'. This extended considerably the discoveries he and his father had earlier made from England. 'Results' includes the double star pairs h 3347 to h 5449 and Innes was later to comment: "The sections on double stars in this work are to the southern heavens what Struve's 'Mensurae Micrometricae' are to the northern hemisphere" (ref. 4).

Of the many deep-sky objects observed, Herschel seems to have been particularly impressed by the η Carinae (then η Argus) nebula. On his chart of this object he was able to plot 1203 stars and wrote, in the 'Results': ".... nor is it easy for language to convey a full impression of the beauty and sublimity of the spectacle it offers when viewed in a sweep, ushered in as it is by so glorious and innumerable procession of stars". He also was one of the fortunate witnesses to the spectacular

Historical Review

eruption of the η Carinae star which began on 1837 December 16, though he had of course returned to England long before it reached its peak.

In discussing the Magellanic Clouds, in which he catalogued 1163 objects, he recorded that: "The general ground of both consists of large tracts and patches of nebulosity in every stage of resolution, from light irresolvable, in a reflector of 18-inches aperture, up to perfectly separated stars like the Milky Way, and clustering groups sufficiently insulated and condensed to come under the designation of irregular and in some cases pretty rich clusters. But besides these there are also nebulae in abundance and globular clusters in every state of condensation" (ref. 5).

He urged that follow-up investigations be carried out but there was little in the way of immediate action so that, as late as 1905, the well-known populariser of astronomy of the time, Sir Robert Ball, was able to sum up knowledge of the Magellanic Clouds in the following words: "It can hardly be doubted that the two nubeculae, which are, roughly speaking, round, or, rather, oval, are not formed accidentally by a vast number of very different objects being ranged at various distances along the same line of sight, but that they really represent two great systems of objects, widely different in constitution, which are here congregated in each other's neighbourhood. There appears to be some essential difference between the clouds of Magellan and the Milky Way, with which the mere naked-eye view would otherwise lead us to associate them" (ref. 2).

Another active observer in the early part of the last century was James Dunlop, who accompanied Sir Thomas Brisbane to New South Wales in 1821 and was made assistant under Charles Rümker, at the observatory founded by him at Paramatta. Dunlop was put in sole charge of the observatory in 1823. Using a 9-foot (2.7 m.) focal length reflector he produced 'A Catalogue of Nebulae and Clusters of Stars in the Southern Hemisphere, observed at Paramatta in New South Wales' which was presented on his behalf to the Royal Society by Sir John Herschel and read on 1827 December 20. The catalogue records 629 southern nebulae and clusters and for this he was awarded the gold medal of the Royal Astronomical Society, the presentation being made by Herschel, who praised Dunlop's qualities as an observer. Ironically, it was Herschel who later discovered that about 2/3 of Dunlop's objects could not be reidentified and reluctantly concluded: "a want of sufficient light or defining power in the instrument used by Mr. Dunlop has been the cause of his setting down objects as nebulae where none really exist" (ref. 5). As a result of this, Dreyer did not include Dunlop's observations in the New General Catalogue unless they had been confirmed by the observations at the Cape.

Dunlop was also responsible for the 'Brisbane Catalogue' of 7385

Historical Review

southern stars and a catalogue of 254 double stars, both of which, unfortunately, contained errors of position, largely in Right Ascension. Dunlop resigned as director of the observatory at Paramatta in 1842 and five years later the instruments were removed to Sydney.

Towards the end of the nineteenth century, the role of the 'gentleman scientist' became less important as more sophisticated techniques became available, such as spectroscopy, and astronomy became more and more the province of the national institutions such as universities.

Harvard and Lick in South America

The last years of the nineteenth century also saw the rise of the great American scientific institutions. In 1899, Harvard established a southern observing station at Arequipa, at the foot of El Misti, high in the Peruvian Andes. This was equipped with a 24-inch (61 cm.) rich-field Clark refractor, paid for out of a substantial gift of money given to Harvard by Miss Catherine Bruce of New York.

The major contribution to astronomy made by this instrument was the regular photographic survey of the Magellanic Clouds by Solon I. Bailey, which enabled Miss Henrietta Swan Leavitt to publish, in 1906, a list of 808 variables in the Large Magellanic Cloud (LMC) and 969 in the Small Magellanic Cloud (SMC) – this was an astonishing feat of patience as the work was carried out manually with just an eyepiece. Among these variables were Cepheids in which, Leavitt found, there was a relationship between the apparent magnitude at maximum and the period. Simply, the longer the period the brighter the magnitude. The reason it was possible to determine such a relationship (called the period-luminosity relationship) for the Magellanic Clouds is that all the stars are so far away that the individual differences in distance are negligible. It is clear therefore, that any differences in apparent magnitude must relate to real differences in absolute magnitude. Fortunately, Cepheids are also intrinsically very bright and can be detected over large distances, and as their light-curves are quite distinctive they can be identified in other neighbouring galaxies. This discovery therefore represented the key to the distances of the nearer galaxies once the distance of just a few Cepheids had been found.

In 1927, the Arequipa operation was transferred to Boyden Observatory on Harvard Kopje, near Bloemfontein, South Africa. The Bruce refractor continued to be used until it was replaced in 1952 by a Baker-Schmidt astrograph, jointly sponsored by the observatories of Armagh and Dunsink in Ireland, and Harvard. Boyden became a major astronomical facility, its

Historical Review

60-inch (1.5 m.) Rockefeller reflector having been installed in 1933.

Harvard's great rival at the turn of the century was Lick Observatory and they too found a need for a southern station. As part of a project to determine the motion of the solar system through space it was clear that it would be necessary to have measurements of the radial velocities of stars in the southern hemisphere. Therefore, in 1900, Lick Observatory director W.W. Campbell secured sponsorship for such a project from financier Darius Ogden Mills. Unfortunately, the early stages of the Lick enterprise were dogged by misfortune. The figure of the first mirror was faulty and when the party, led by W.H. Wright, eventually arrived in Valparaiso, Chile, to set up the observatory, their equipment was held up in port by strikes. Having reached the site, the dome to be used was then found to be in a state of disrepair. Eventually, the first observations were made in September 1903.

The observatory, which was set up at Cerro San Cristobal on the outskirts of Santiago, was equipped with a $36\frac{1}{2}$-inch (93 cm.) f/18 silver-on-glass Cassegrain reflector, equipped with a 3-prism spectrograph. The original plan had been to establish the observatory as a short term venture and then return the equipment to the U.S.A.; however, the Lick Observatory Chile Station was found to be so valuable that Mills was persuaded to continue his support until 1911.

Wright returned to Lick in 1906 and his position in Chile was filled for a while by Heber D. Curtis. Financial problems plagued the following years and in 1926 a revolution brought to power an unsympathetic military government. It became more difficult to administer the Chile station so, in 1928, Lick sold the complete observatory to the Catholic University of Chile.

Despite its short life, the results obtained were considerable – over 10,000 radial velocity spectrograms were obtained and many new multiple stars were discovered. Aitken was later to comment that knowledge of southern spectroscopic binaries at the time was almost entirely attributable to the work of this station.

In the 1950's the observatory began to fall into disuse and decay, although restoration was begun in 1980. Even so, its long-term future remains in doubt.

Twentieth Century Astronomy in South Africa

Observatories in South Africa had meanwhile become the centre for much

Historical Review

of the double star research in the southern hemisphere. Dr. R.T.A. Innes joined the staff of the Royal Observatory at the Cape of Good Hope in 1896 after having published lists of 42 new pairs made with a $6\frac{1}{4}$-inch (15.9 cm.) refractor at Sydney, Australia. At the Cape he had access to more substantial equipment and was able to continue his work using 7-inch (17.8 cm.) and 18-inch (45.7 cm.) refractors, bringing his total of discoveries to 432 pairs.

Innes became Government Astronomer at the Union Observatory, Johannesburg in 1903, which gave him access to a 9-inch (22.9 cm.) refractor, and in 1909 he was able to order a $26\frac{1}{2}$-inch (67.3 cm.) f/16 refractor from Grubb in England. This proved to be a fine instrument when installed, even though it was not actually delivered until 1925! One can imagine the frustration Innes must have felt during the intervening years.

The staff of the Union Observatory was soon enhanced by the recruitment of Willem H. van den Bos and W.S. Finsen. A systematic double star survey of the southern hemisphere was begun which resulted in the following discoveries: Innes - 1613 pairs, Finsen - 300 pairs and van den Bos - over 2000 pairs.

At about the same time, the Lamont-Hussey Observatory was established at Bloemfontein, equipped with a 27-inch (68.6 cm.) Brashear refractor. Double star studies played a prominent part in the use of this instrument also and the capable observers at the observatory, Rossiter, Jessup and Donner, discovered 1961, 1424 and 1327 pairs respectively.

The $26\frac{1}{2}$-inch at the Union Observatory is now under used. It has never been modernised and is still operated by purely mechanical systems. In addition, its site has been virtually swallowed up by the expanding suburbs of Johannesburg. Even so, in 1982, when Webb Society Vice-President R.W. Argyle had the opportunity to use the instrument, he was able to confirm for himself the excellent quality of the Grubb objective, measuring the extremely close double, Finsen 357, at 0".18.

Astronomy in South Africa was enhanced after World War II when the Radcliffe Observatory moved from Oxford, England to a site near Pretoria in 1948, installing a 74-inch (1.88 m.) reflector, which at the time was the largest instrument in the southern hemisphere. This telescope proved to be very productive, averaging over 2400 hours use per year in its first quarter-century, according to Dr. Andrew D. Thackeray, who was Director of the observatory from 1950 to 1974.

Historical Review

In 1952, Thackeray and A.J. Wesselink used the 74-inch in showing that the distances to the Magellanic Clouds had been underestimated by a factor of two. It was also used to establish the stellar composition of the Clouds and other galaxies.

When South African astronomy was reorganised in 1972, the 74-inch was moved to Sutherland in the Karoo to form part of the new South African Astronomical Observatory (S.A.A.O.), together with 40-inch (1.02 m.), 30-inch (76 cm.) and 20-inch (51 cm.) reflectors. Dr. Thackeray continued to make regular observations until his untimely death in a road accident in 1978.

Modern Southern Observatories

Considering the importance of, the southern skies it is perhaps surprising that really large instruments and sophisticated observatories did not make an appearance until the mid-1970's, the main centres having been in South Africa and at Mount Stromlo, near Canberra, Australia, where the main instrument is a 74-inch reflector. This site also has six other instruments, including 50-inch (1.27 m.), 40-inch (1.02 m.) and 30-inch (76 cm.) reflectors.

Research is now concentrated in two geographical areas:

1. Northern Chile –

(a) Cerro Tololo Inter-American Observatory (CTIO) – situated at an elevation of 2400 m. on Cerro Tololo, this observatory is administered by the organisation of American universities (AURA) which controls the Kitt Peak National Observatory and has, as its main instrument, a 4.0 m. reflector – currently the largest telescope in the southern hemisphere – which began operations in 1976.

(b) European Southern Observatory (ESO) – some 74 km. north of CTIO, the ESO is situated at an altitude of 2400 m. at La Silla, in the Atacama region of the Chilean Andes. The ESO organisation was formed in 1962 by West Germany, The Netherlands, Belgium, Sweden, Denmark and France and the observatory now boasts a comprehensive array of instruments:

        3.6 m. reflector (+ 1.5 m. auxillary)
        1.0 m. Schmidt
        1.5 m. reflector
        1.0 m. reflector
        Double astrograph (40 & 25 cm.)

Historical Review

plus several minor instruments. The 3.6 m. saw 'first light' on 1976
November 7.

(c) Carnegie Southern Observatory (CARSO) - lying about 24 km. north-west
of the ESO complex, at La Serena, the southern station of the Carnegie
Institute of Washington has, as its primary instrument, the 2.5 m. Du Pont
reflector. There are also 1.0 m. and 60 cm. reflectors. This observatory
is associated with the Mount Wilson observatory in California.

2. New South Wales, Australia -

(a) Anglo-Australian Observatory (AAO) - see below.

(b) United Kingdom Schmidt Telescope (UKST) - less than 1 km. from the
Anglo-Australian Telescope (AAT), the UKST was built and is operated by
the Royal Observatory, Edinburgh (ROE). The telescope began work in 1973
and, although virtually the twin of the 1.2 m. Palomar Schmidt, it has
benefitted from the combination of a dark site and advances in optical and
photographic technology which give it superior performance. Stars as
faint as about magnitude 23 can be found on its 14-inch (35.6 cm.) square
plates. The AAT/UKST site also has 40-inch (1.02 m.), 24-inch (61 cm.)
and 16-inch (40.6 cm.) reflectors.

The Anglo-Australian Telescope

   Though most of the major southern observatories have been very briefly
described, it may be of interest to look at just one in a little more
detail, the AAT, which has the reputation of having one of the most
advanced instruments in the world and is constantly at the forefront of
research in the exploration of the southern sky.

   The AAT project began in 1967 with an agreement by the U.K. and
Australian governments to build a large aperture reflector, similar in
design to that already established at Kitt Peak in the U.S.A. The cost of
construction and operation were to be shared equally, as was observing
time. The site chosen for the new observatory was at Siding Spring
Mountain near Coonabarabran, New South Wales.

   The figuring of the 3.89 m. primary mirror was carried out by the
British firm of Grubb Parsons & Co. and it was aluminised late in 1974.
The important telescope mounting and control systems were built by
Mitsubishi Electric of Japan. Construction and assembly of the buildings
and equipment took place in time for observations to begin in early 1975.

Historical Review

The telescope can be used at Prime focus (f/3.3), Cassegrain focus (f/8 or f/15) and Coude focus (f/36).

As well as having a particularly good mirror, the drive and control systems are of an advanced design, and the AAT was the first large telescope to have computer control of all routine operations. Other computers are dedicated to the acquisition and on-line reduction of data. A Digital Equipment VAX 11/780 computer system has also been installed to help with data reduction and analysis. Amongst other things, this system enables TV images obtained via the telescope to be manipulated to enhance detail and specific features of an object under study.

Instrumentation for use with the telescope is also 'state-of-the-art'. The first CCD camera, which came into use at the prime focus of the telescope in 1981, was found to be capable of extending the South Galactic Pole photoelectric magnitude sequence to B = 23.5. Other instruments used with the AAT include the Image Photon Counting System (IPCS) developed by Dr. Alec Boksenberg of the Royal Greenwich Observatory, an Infrared Photometer-Spectrometer (IRPS) and the remarkable TAURUS device, essentially a tunable ultra-fine filter which can examine spectrum bandwidths as narrow as 0.1 Å.

Astronomers at the AAT have been responsible for many important discoveries and the development of new techniques, for example in astro-photography; one result of this has been the identification of a class of elliptical galaxy surrounded by a series of low contrast symmetrical 'shells'. One of these galaxies, NGC 3923, has 16 known shells.

The Future

Improvements in southern astronomical facilities, like those in the northern hemisphere, seem likely to be more along the lines of developments in the auxillary equipment to extract more data using the telescopes already available, rather than in the construction of new large instruments. Devices such as the IPCS and TAURUS have proved their worth and more are being developed. For example, for use with the Isaac Newton Telescope on La Palma, RGO scientists have developed an image stabilizer, a moving mirror which will compensate for a star's apparent motion in an unsteady atmosphere, resulting in an image which may be as sharp as 0.3 arc-seconds (which compares favourably with the Hubble Space Telescope, which is expected to produce 0.1 arc-second resolution).

Certainly, the age of the single-mirror large telescope seems to be on the wane with the advent of computer-controlled multiple-mirror telescopes.

Historical Review

The prototype MMT was opened on Mt. Hopkins, Arizona in 1979. This uses six lightweight 1.8 m., $f/2$ mirrors mounted together to give the light collecting power equivalent to a single 4.5 m. mirror telescope. Also in the U.S.A.,plans are already being laid for the construction of a 15 m. MMT (called the National New Technology Telescope (NNTT)), consisting of four 7.5 m. mirrors. In the southern hemisphere, the ESO is developing a Very Large Telescope (VLT) which is expected to be made up of an array of four 8 m. instruments that could be operated individually or as an interferometer.

. . . .

References

1. Lacaille; 'On the Nebulous Stars of the Southern Sky', Memoires de l'Academie des Sciences, 1755, pp. 286 - 296.

2. Ball, R.S.; 'The Story of the Heavens', Cassell & Co., 1905.

3. Buttman, G.; 'The Shadow of the Telescope', C. Scribner, 1970.

4. Aitken, R.G.; 'The Binary Stars', Dover Publ. Inc., 1964.

5. Herschel, J.F.W.; 'Results of Astronomical Observations made during the Years 1834, 5, 6, 7, 8 at the Cape of Good Hope', Smith, Elder & Co. 1847.

Other source material used in the compilation of this section is listed in the general Bibilography, at the rear of this volume.

PART TWO

EXTENDED DESCRIPTIONS
OF SELECTED OBJECTS

Extended Descriptions

NGC 55: SCULPTOR

NGC 55 is an important member of the Sculptor Group (also called the South Galactic Pole Group) of galaxies, one of the closest aggregations beyond our own Local Group. Because of the proximity of the Sculptor Group, the distances to individual members vary significantly as a proportion of the overall distance, and NGC 55 is in the foreground at a distance of only 9.5 million light-years.

With a size of 25' x 4' it is a highly elongated system and is obviously an edge-on galaxy. It has been classified as type Sc but it appears to be somewhat irregular. There is no distinct nuclear bulge and the well resolved 'bar', which forms the body of the galaxy, is by no means entirely symmetrical.

Observing NGC 55 with the Yale 1.0 m. reflector at CTIO, and using a 16Å passband filter, Graham & Lawrie (ref. 1) have discovered a huge nebulous loop about 2' east of the centre of the galaxy. This loop is probably part of a 'shell' or 'bubble' which may be as large as 3000 light-years in diameter. It is suggested that the bubble began as an envelope of gas and dust around a massive OB association or cluster which began expanding because of radiation pressure. The continuing expansion could be maintained by radiation pressure from other stars swallowed up by the expanding bubble. This feature is not visible to visual examination or even using normal photographic techniques.

....

NGC 253: SCULPTOR

Though often considered to be a purely southern object, NGC 253 was in fact discovered by Caroline Herschel from England in 1783. It is the brightest member of the Sculptor Group of galaxies and lies at a distance of some 12 million light-years.

In apparent size, NGC 253 is 22' x 6' and, though rather more dusty, bears some comparison with the Andromeda Galaxy in the northern hemisphere. Inclined at 12° to the line of sight, similar to Andromeda, its spiral structure can be discerned, although this is rather more chaotic and mottled, and its nuclear region is nothing like as conspicuous.

There is some evidence of explosive activity in the nuclear region and material is being ejected at velocities up to 120 km/s. The nucleus contains a considerable mass of dust and gas and emits most of its energy

Extended Descriptions

at IR wavelengths, making NGC 253 the third brightest IR galaxy in the sky. It is also the radio source PKS 0045-25.

. . . .

SMALL MAGELLANIC CLOUD (SMC)

The SMC is the smaller of the two major satellites of our own Galaxy and lies at a distance of about 200,000 light-years, in the constellation of Tucana. It is an irregular galaxy of type Im IV-V and in visual appearance, rather pear-shaped. The main body of the galaxy is about $3\frac{1}{2}^{\circ}$ in its greatest extent, although on deep photographs it has been found to be about $9^{\circ} \times 8^{\circ}$. With an absolute magnitude of -16.8 the SMC is sixth brightest of the 29 known galaxies in the Local Group. It has a mass of about one thousand million Suns.

In contrast with the richness of the LMC, the SMC is a rather poor object, with few significant areas of nebulosity and less galactic and globular clusters (note that the nearby bright globulars NGC 104 (47 Tuc.) and NGC 362 are not associated with the SMC). However, at the northern end of the SMC is a massive chain of clusters and nebulosity which includes NGC 346, 371 and 395, with NGC 330 close by. These and other SMC objects are shown on the chart at Appendix 3, which also includes a listing of other interesting objects in this galaxy. The brightest individual star in the SMC is HD 7583 at m_v = 10.1.

Australian astronomers Mathewson and Ford (ref. 2) have found, using the 64 m. radiotelescope at Parkes, that the neutral hydrogen in the area has two distinctly preferred Doppler shifts, separated by 30 km/s. This difference is also found in the radial velocities of other objects, such as individual stars, planetary nebulae and HII regions. It has been suggested that the reason for this is that, in fact, what we perceive to be a single galaxy is in reality two galaxies, one almost directly behind the other. The nearest, and most massive, has been termed the 'Small Magellanic Cloud Remnant' (SMCR) and the furthest the 'Mini-Magellanic Cloud' (MMC). The SMCR is concentrated on the main body of the observed galaxy (at approximately R.A. 00h. 50m., Dec. -73° (2000)) and the MMC more to the north-east (at approximately R.A. 01h. 05m., Dec. -72° (2000)).

From theoretical considerations it has been known for a while that the LMC and SMC underwent a close encounter some 200 million years ago and it may be that the SMC was torn apart by the forces involved.

. . . .

Extended Descriptions

THE FORNAX CLUSTER OF GALAXIES

The Fornax Cluster, on the border of Fornax and Eridanus, contains eighteen NGC members and a number of minor constituents. It is comparatively close by, at an estimated distance of 65 million light-years (20 Mpc.).

Dominating the cluster is NGC 1316, classified as type Sa pec. (mag. 10.5). On first glance it appears to be an ordinary elliptical galaxy but closer examination shows a complex of dust patches and lanes, mostly at the periphery of the bright oval central region. So odd are these markings that Shapley (ref. 3), on examining a detailed plate of the galaxy, taken with the 60-inch Rockefeller reflector, discarded it, marking the envelope 'defective image of NGC 1316'!

NGC 1316 is also the radio source Fornax A and is considered to be a prime example of a galaxy merger. Deep photographs show that its elliptical-like body is embedded in an extensive envelope which has a complicated structure. There is a series of 'shells' or 'ripples' in the envelope on which are superimposed curved streamers and other projections. Theoretical considerations show that this state of affairs could have been brought about by a small disc galaxy having merged with the main body about 1 Gyr. ago. This interpretation of the phenomena exhibited by NGC 1316 is also supported by other observational evidence, such as the presence of a highly inclined gas disc which rotates much faster than the stars and which would be difficult to explain otherwise.

NGC 1399 is the second brightest galaxy in the Fornax Cluster and is easily identified because of the presence of NGC 1404 just 8' to the south. Third brightest is NGC 1365, a beautiful face-on barred spiral. This galaxy is a giant in its class with a diameter of 65 kpc and total absolute magnitude -21.6. The spectral features of its nuclear region reveal its Seyfert 1 character.

Another interesting galaxy in this cluster is NGC 1386, which is possibly the nearest type 2 Seyfert galaxy.

An identification chart for galaxies in the central part of the Fornax Cluster is shown on page 18. The galaxies NGC 1386, 1389 and 1437 are actually in the constellation of Eridanus.

....

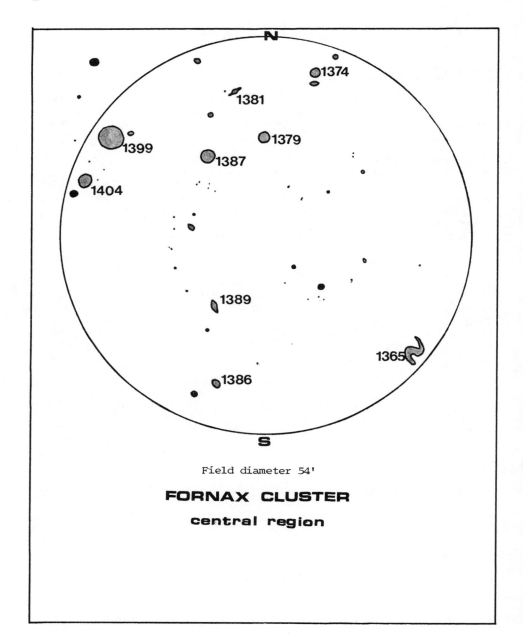

Field diameter 54'

FORNAX CLUSTER

central region

Extended Descriptions

LARGE MAGELLANIC CLOUD (LMC)

Some 22° away from the SMC, the LMC is a splendid object in the
southern skies, appearing as a detached portion of the Milky Way. Of
course, we now know that the LMC is a galaxy in its own right, a barred
spiral of type SBm III. Close to our own Galaxy, at a distance of only
160,000 light-years, it is tidally distorted and its spiral arms are
quite inconspicuous, although one has been traced out as a faint streamer
20° long. In the Local Group of galaxies the LMC is fourth brightest
(absolute magnitude -18.5) and is only slightly less luminous than M.33
(absolute magnitude -18.9). The mass of the LMC is about 6 thousand
million times that of the Sun.

Most of the light and mass of the LMC is concentrated in and around
the bar, and even with a small instrument this galaxy is a rich
aggregation of stars, clusters and nebulae of astonishing complexity.

Surveys of the stellar content show there to be over 200,000 stars
brighter than M_v -1.5, and of these the most brilliant is perhaps
S Doradus in the LMC galactic cluster NGC 1910. This cluster also
includes several other super-luminous stars. S Doradus is variable, and
even at the distance of the LMC is of apparent magnitude 8.4 - 9.5. It
has a spectrum of the P Cygni type, with bright hydrogen lines. The
luminosity of S Doradus must be in the order of 500,000 Suns, although
it may be that it is not, in fact, just a single star.

Another important system in the LMC is the OB association, involved
with the nebulous region NGC 1936, which Shapley called 'Constellation I'.
This complex is about 500 light-years across and the total mass of stars
and ionised gas may be about 100,000 Suns, with possibly another 5 million
solar masses of neutral hydrogen surrounding it out to a radius of 500
light-years.

Over 500 planetary nebulae, supernova remnants and gas 'bubbles' are
known. These bubbles are only a comparatively recently recognised
phenomenon and, in the LMC, are typified by the object N.70. This is a
complicated nebulous ring, resembling a SNR, in which is a small cluster
of stars, one being of the Wolf-Rayet variety or similar, exhibiting
an intense stellar wind. The bubble, which in the case of N.70 is some
360 light-years in diameter, is formed at the interface between the
stellar wind and the surrounding hydrogen gas in the interstellar medium.

Undoubtedly, the single most interesting object in the LMC is the

Extended Descriptions

giant HII region NGC 2070 (also called the 'Tarantula Nebula' or the
'30 Doradus Nebula'). This is a vast area of ionised gas almost 900
light-years in diameter, having a mass of 500,000 Suns. Burnham (ref. 4)
points out that if it were as close to us as the Orion Nebula it would
cover 30° of sky and shine with a brightness three times greater than
Venus.

The powerhouse of this object, which is one of the largest of its type
known in the Universe, is a massive cluster of over 100 supergiant stars
at its centre. The foremost among these is R136 (= HD 38268), which
detailed optical studies seem to show is made up of three components, the
most significant being R136a. This object has recently been the subject
of considerable controversy because, if this is indeed a single star, as
speckle observations would indicate, it is a record breaker in almost
every conceivable respect, with a mass greater than 2000 Suns and a
luminosity of about 50 million Suns! Such a star is unprecedented and
would clearly be very unstable. Some investigators take the view that
R136a is really a densely packed group of perhaps 8 - 10 O and WR stars,
the speckle observations being invalidated by the complex background.

A chart of the LMC, indicating major objects, is shown at Appendix 2,
together with a listing of other interesting features.

....

NGC 3372 and η CARINAE

The star η Carinae is first recorded in Bayer's 1603 'Uranometria' as
an object of 4th magnitude. Halley found it to be of similar brightness
in 1677.

The star varied spectacularly during the nineteenth century, reaching
first magnitude during its outburst of 1827. It then faded before
returning to a similar brightness in the early 1830's. However, on 1837
December 16, John Herschel was astonished to find that η Carinae had
risen to a magnitude greater than that of Rigel. Unfortunately, having to
return to England in 1838 he was unable to follow it throughout its full
increase. Eventually the star peaked in March 1843 at -0.9, second only
to Sirius in brightness. Correcting for its estimated distance of 6800
light-years, its true brightness must have been about 6 million Suns.
By 1867, η Carinae had faded to about magnitude 6, and is now about
magnitude 8, although there have been slight revivals in 1941 and 1952.

As a result of this extraordinary behaviour, Zwicky, in 1965, was

Extended Descriptions

prompted to classify it as an exceptional type of supernova (Type V).

The η Carinae star is immediately involved in a tiny (about 12" x 8") dense nebula called the 'Homunculus', which has the appearance of a human figure. This nebula is expanding at about 500 km/s, and since it was observed by Innes at the turn of the century, the tiny knots which he assumed to be companion stars have gradually expanded and become more diffuse. These knots may be the debris of the activity of the 1840's.

The star and the 'Homunculus' nebula are embedded in the extensive NGC 3372 nebula which is over 1° in diameter. This was discovered by Lacaille in 1751. Dark rifts and patches are found all across this nebulosity and one particularly conspicuous dark lane has given it the name 'Keyhole Nebula'.

As well as η Carinae itself, the nebula also includes several other hot, massive stars, particularly HD 93129A, the brightest member of the cluster Trumpler 14, which is part of an OB aggregate that also includes the clusters Cr. 228, Tr. 16 and Tr. 15. The two very red supergiant variables in the region, RT and BO Carinae, appear to be associated with Tr. 15. It should be noted that the clusters NGC 3293 and NGC 3324, which are also nearby, are foreground objects at perhaps only half the distance of the η Carinae complex.

The η Carinae star is apparently a very massive object and its evolution is consequently very rapid. Several investigators have suggested that it may be nearing the end of its life, and may erupt as a supernova in the comparatively near future. At its assumed distance, such a supernova would probably attain a magnitude of −5 so that, for a short while, it would be brighter than any object in the sky except the Sun and Moon.

. . . .

NGC 5128: CENTAURUS

At a distance of 16 million light-years, NGC 5128 is the nearest of the giant radio galaxies, having been discovered to be a radio source by Bolton in 1947. Curiously, until about that time it was still being classified by some authorities as a peculiar nebula in our own Galaxy.

Visually, it appears almost spherical with a conspicuous and highly complex lane of dust encircling the galaxy around its equator. Baade and Minkowski believed the chaotic appearance was due to 2 galaxies in

Extended Descriptions

collision, and more recently massive explosive activity in the centre was
blamed. Like NGC 1316 however, it is now considered to be a prime
example of a galaxy merger, a small gas-rich disc companion having fallen
into the giant spherical system many millions of years ago. Evidence in
support of this includes the presence of a warped gaseous disc which
rotates at a considerably greater rate than the stellar part of the
system. There are some remaining visible signs of this event in the
existence of 'ripples' in the extensions of the visible galaxy which are
found on deep photographs, such as those by Cannon with the UKST. These
faint extensions make the greatest optical extent of the galaxy about
$1^{o}.2$.

The associated radio source, Centaurus A, is 6° x 10° and the emission
is concentrated in two lobes, one either side of the visible galaxy, and
at right angles to the dust lane. Two smaller areas of emission are
found along the same axis but much closer in, superimposed on the
extensions to the visible galaxy.

At the centre of NGC 5128 is a large cluster of stars and gas with a
luminosity of perhaps 100 thousand million Suns. The core of this
cluster contains a compact source of IR and X-ray as well as radio
emission. The X-ray source is variable by a factor of 3 or 4 over a
period of about 5 years and exhibits regular flares.

There is also an X-ray jet, containing several knots, several arc-
minutes long, which was discovered by the orbiting Einstein observatory.
The jet points to one of the radio lobes and is also associated with an
optical jet or filament discovered some time previously.

This remarkable galaxy is classified as type SO + S pec. and contains
one more curious anomaly: it has not been possible positively to
identify the presence of even a single globular cluster with it. The
similarly massive system M.87, on the other hand, has several thousand.
The reason for this discrepancy is not known, but could be a consequence
of its eventful history.

. . . .

NGC 5139 (ω CENTAURI)

Visible to the unaided eye, this globular cluster was discovered to
be non-stellar by Halley in 1677. It is 16,500 light-years distant and may
be the most massive globular associated with our Galaxy. Certainly, it has
the largest diameter of any known globular, 620 light-years. Unlike most

Extended Descriptions

globulars, it is distinctly non-spherical, possibly due to rotation.

Woolley and Candy (ref. 5) have calculated its orbit about the Galaxy, and find it to be retrograde. It loops around the centre in a three-petalled roseate pattern from a close point of 6200 light-years out to 21,000 light-years.

NGC 5139 is estimated to be about 15 thousand million years old, and as a result of this extreme age, the stars have a low percentage of metals in their make-up. The brightest are red giants which are of apparent magnitude 11. How many stars there are altogether in the cluster is not known, though one estimate suggests two million. At the centre, the density of stars may be 25,000 times greater than in the solar neighbourhood. The night sky of any planet in this region would be an amazing sight!

....

NGC 5236 (M.83): HYDRA

This galaxy is another of Lacaille's discoveries from the Cape of Good Hope, being found in 1752. It was later described by Messier who found it to be a very faint, starless nebula.

Modern photographs show it to be a superb face-on spiral of type SBc(s)II. Perhaps its most remarkable feature is its system of well defined, massive spiral arms, seemingly alive with luminous blue supergiant stars and bright HII regions, giving the impression of a rapidly whirling vortex. Like another 'massive-arm' spiral (NGC 6946 in Cepheus), NGC 5236 has a high rate of supernova production, five having been found to date, in 1923, 1950, 1957, 1968 and 1983.

NGC 5236 is all the more spectacular because of its proximity, being only 10 million light-years away. It appears to be part of a small group of galaxies which includes the other peculiar galaxies NGC 5128 (Cen A) and NGC 5253.

Deep red Schmidt plates show the presence of very faint arc-like structures and HII regions out to 40 kpc. These are associated with the vast HI envelope which surrounds the galaxy.

....

Extended Descriptions

NGC 6514 (M.20) 'TRIFID NEBULA': SAGITTARIUS

NGC 6514 is a lovely, red, rosette-shaped nebula, broken by three dark lanes, which give it its popular name. At the centre there appear to be two bright stars: a closer examination, however, reveals that four stars are actually present, two of which are spectroscopic binaries.

The object mainly responsible for ionising the nebula is the O8 star HD 164492. The UV light from this star breaks up the hydrogen atoms which subsequently recombine, emitting red light at the $H\alpha$ wavelength (6563$\overset{o}{A}$). A particularly distinctive feature of this nebula is the beautiful combination of the red rosette and the nearby blue reflection nebula (deep photographs show that it actually surrounds the rosette). The source of the reflection nebula is the F5 star HD 164514; being rather cooler than HD 164492 its ionising potential is not as great so it illuminates the nebulosity through forward scattering of light.

M.8 is in the same rich-field as the Trifid Nebula and may well be part of the same nebula complex. Certainly, the two objects appear to be at similar distances (about 4500 light-years).

. . . .

NGC 6523/30 (M.8) LAGOON NEBULA: SAGITTARIUS

The Lagoon Nebula is a large, bright nebula/star cluster complex of intricate structure. It can be seen with the unaided eye as a nebulous spot of about magnitude 5, and was apparently first recorded by Hodierna around 1654, though he may have seen only the cluster. The actual nebulosity was recorded by Le Gentil in 1749 and Lacaille in 1752.

Even low power equipment will show that the nebulosity divides into three areas of brightness, within an overall oval form about 1° across. The brightest part of the nebula is near the stars 9 and 7 Sgr., which are members of the involved cluster (NGC 6530). At the centre of the bright region is a tiny intense nebula called the 'Hourglass'. Adjacent to this is the O9 star Herschel 36, which is the source of its illumination and may have been formed as recently as 10,000 years ago.

Photographs show that the nebula is a beautiful deep red colour and is apparently ionised by just three O stars, 9 Sgr., H. 36, and HD 165052.

Lada et al. have proposed that NGC 6530, along with many similar objects, formed just inside a giant molecular cloud (GMC) and subsequently caused a 'blister' on its surface which enables us to see 'inside' at the ionised part of the cloud (ref. 6).

....

NGC 7293: AQUARIUS

NGC 7293 (PK 36-57°1), is the planetary nebula with the largest apparent angular diameter, about $\frac{1}{2}^\circ$, as great as the full Moon! Detailed photographs show it to have a beautiful annular structure, with radial streaks pointing to the central star. These streaks, which are especially prominent on red photographs, include numerous tiny knots or condensations, which are typically 1" - 3" across and represent features roughly 150 A.U. in diameter at the nebula's assumed distance of about 400 light-years. The distance of NGC 7293, in common with most other planetary nebulae, is by no means accurately known.

The annulus shows evidence of some stratification, which gives rise to its popular name, the Helix Nebula. In some publications the object is also called the Sunflower Nebula, a name derived from the radial streaks.

Photographic amplification of red plates of the nebula reveal that it is rather more extensive than classical depictions would indicate. Well beyond the annulus is a complex series of huge loops and filaments which more than double its apparent size and give it the twin lobed symmetry of a bi-polar nebula. This may be evidence of activity in the atmosphere of the central star which occurred prior to the ejection of the shell which has given rise to the annulus.

The central star of NGC 7293 is a tiny white dwarf (type sdO) with an apparent magnitude of 13.4 and surface temperature of about 95,000° K.

....

References

1. ----------; Sky & Telescope, September 1982, p. 228.

2. ----------; Sky & Telescope, April 1984, p. 317.

3. Hodge, P.W.; 'An Early Photograph of Fornax A', Sky & Telescope, June 1975, p. 354.

Extended Descriptions

4. Burnham, R.; 'Burnham's Celestial Handbook - Vol. 2', p. 851, Dover Publ. Inc., 1978.

5. Murdin, P. & Allen, D.A.; 'Catalogue of the Universe', p. 136, Cambridge University Press, 1979.

6. Solomon, P. & Edmunds, M.; 'Giant Molecular Clouds in the Galaxy (Third Gregynog Astrophysics Workshop)', p. 239, Pergamon Press, 1980.

PART THREE

CATALOGUE OF OBSERVATIONS

Catalogue

Introduction

This catalogue contains observations of southern deep-sky objects made
by Webb Society members, using the unaided eye and instruments from 12x40
binoculars to telescopes of 158-inches (4.0 m.) aperture.

The catalogue is divided into six sections:

1. Open clusters
2. Globular clusters
3. Planetary nebulae
4. Diffuse nebulae
5. Galaxies
6. LMC/SMC objects.

In each section the written observations are presented first, followed by
a selection of drawings, which, to conform with the standard astronomical
convention, are orientated with North at the bottom and South at the top.

For ease of reference, priority has been given to NGC numerical order
rather than strict R.A. listing.

As well as written descriptions and drawings other relevant
observational details are also presented. Positions quoted are for Epoch
2000.0. At the beginning of each section, more information is given as to
the specific types of data provided with each object in that section.
Also given is a list of the objects contained there plus the initials of
the respective observers, which can be referred back to the following
table for the observer's name, observing site and instruments used.

Observers

The work of the following observers has been used in the compilation
of the catalogue:

D.A. Allen	Siding Spring, N.S.W., Australia	154-inch (3.9 m.)
	Mt. Wilson, Ca., U.S.A.	100-inch (2.5 m.)
		60-inch (1.5 m.)
	Sutherland, Cape Prov., S. Africa	40-inch (1.0 m.)
E.S. Barker	Herne Bay, Kent, U.K.	8½-inch (21.6 cm.)

Catalogue

D. & B. Branchett	St. Augustine, Fla., U.S.A.	6-inch (15.2 cm.)
	Deltona, Fla., U.S.A.	5-inch (12.7 cm.)
		15 x 80 bin.
P. Brennan	Regina, Sask., Canada	8-inch (20.3 cm.)
		6-inch (15.2 cm.)
R.J. Buta	Cerro Tololo, Chile	158-inch (4.0 m.)
		40-inch (1.0 m.)
		36-inch (91 cm.)
	Siding Spring, N.S.W., Australia	40-inch (1.0 m.)
		24-inch (61 cm.)
		16-inch (41 cm.)
	Mt. Stromlo, A.C.T., Australia	6-inch (15.2 cm.)
	Mc Donald Obs., Tx., U.S.A.	30-inch (76 cm.)
J. Corder	Asheville, N.C., U.S.A.	17½-inch (44.5 cm.)
	Tice, Fla., U.S.A.	12½-inch (32 cm.)
		8-inch (20.3 cm.)
		6-inch (15.2 cm.)
		4¼-inch (10.5 cm.)
D. Dutton	Christchurch, New Zealand	13.1-inch (33.3 cm.)
C. Foster	Hillcrest, Natal, S. Africa	4½-inch (11.2 cm.)
C. Henshaw	Kadoma, Zimbabwe	12-inch (30.5 cm.)
		12 x 40 bin.
V. Hirsch	Port Elizabeth, S. Africa	6-inch (15.2 cm.)
		4½-inch (11.2 cm.)
		2¼-inch O.G. (6.0 cm.)
G.M. Hurst	Earls Barton, Northants, U.K.	10-inch (25.4 cm.)
S.J. Hynes	Crewe, Ches., U.K.	8½-inch (21.6 cm.)
	Negombo, Sri Lanka	4¼-inch RFT (10.5 cm.)
	Playa de las Americas, Tenerife	
	Rethymnon, Crete	
K. Glyn Jones	Johannesburg, S. Africa	12½-inch (32 cm.)
	Winkfield, Berks., U.K.	8-inch (20.3 cm.)

Catalogue

R.J. Morales	Tucson, Az., U.S.A.	13.1-inch (33.3 cm.)
		10-inch (25.4 cm.)
		8-inch (20.3 cm.)
		6-inch (15.2 cm.)
C. Nugent	Pontefract, W. Yorks, U.K.	8½-inch (21.6 cm.)
J. Perkins	Kirkby-in-Ashfield, Notts., U.K.	10-inch (25.4 cm.)
S. Selleck	Santa Barbara, Ca., U.S.A.	10-inch (25.4 cm.)
		8-inch (20.3 cm.)
M.J. Thomson	Santa Barbara, Ca., U.S.A.	16½-inch (42 cm.)

Catalogue

SECTION 1: OPEN CLUSTERS

Data provided with this section:

(a) Catalogue number
(b) R.A. and Dec. for Epoch 2000.0
(c) Apparent magnitude
(d) Angular diameter
(e) Trumpler type
(f) Constellation

The data in (c) to (e) is based on the Lund-Strasbourg catalogue as described by G. Lyngå (Astron. Data Cen. Bul., 2, 1981) and supplemented by information from Atlas Coeli (Becvar, 1964). In a number of cases, additional information will be found on the line below the basic data. Note: a brief explanation of the Trumpler classification system is given in Volume 3 of the 'Handbook', page 7.

Observers and Accredited Objects

NGC 2017 – VH, SJH	NGC 2910 – VH	NGC 5999 – JC, VH
2204 – PB	2925 – DD	6025 – VH
2287 – SJH	2972 – DD	6152 – JC
Rup 8 – GH	3033 – DD, VH	6193 – VH
NGC 2360 – PB	3105 – DAA	6204 – JC
2362 – JC, SJH	3114 – JC, VH, CF	6231 – VH, JC, SJH
2367 – JC, PB	3228 – JC, VH	6242 – SJH
Asterism – SJH	3293 – JC, VH	Tr. 24 – VH, SJH
NGC 2383 – PB	IC 2602 – VH, CH	NGC 6268 – JC
2421 – GH	NGC 3532 – JC, VH, CH	6281 – VH
2422 – SJH, JC	3603 – VH	6322 – JC, SJH
2437 – SJH	Mel.105 – VH	IC 4651 – VH
2439 – SJH	NGC 3766 – VH	NGC 6383 – JC
2447 – JC, SJH	3909 – JC	6405 – JC, SJH
2451 – SJH	3960 – JC	6475 – JC, SJH
2453 – JC, GH	Rup 98 – DAA	6520 – JC
Tr. 9 – GH	NGC 4052 – DAA, DD	6531 – JC, SJH
NGC 2489 – SJH	4103 – DAA, JC	6540 – VH
2516 – VH, CF, CH	4349 – DAA, DD	6568 – KGJ
2527 – PB	4439 – DAA, DD	Tr. 32 – GH
2547 – DD, JC, VH	4609 – DAA, DD	NGC 6611 – SJH, JC
2660 – VH	4755 – KGJ, VH, CF	6613 – SJH
IC 2395 – VH	5299 – JC, VH	IC 4725 – SJH
NGC 2671 – JC	5460 – JC	NGC 6645 – PB
2818A – JC, DD	5823 – JC	

Catalogue	R.A.	Dec.	mag.	A.D.	Type	Const.
NGC 2017	05 39.4	−17 51				Lep

RNGC Class 7 object.

---

(6) An interesting group of 8 stars in an almost circular pattern. Nearby is a group of 4 more stars. Brightest stars about mag. 8.
(4¼ RFT) A small cluster, perhaps only 10' across. Three stars well seen plus three or four much fainter ones. In same 3° field as α Lep.

NGC 2204	06 15.7	−18 36	9.6	10	II 2 r	CMa

---

(8) Inconspicuous at low power but easy at x125. Contains 25 − 30 stars, the brightest being of about mag. 11. Main body of the cluster is about 6' x 3' but with outliers this is increased to about 10' diameter.

NGC 2287 M.41	06 47.0	−20 45	5.0	40	II 3 m	CMa

(8½) Large cluster of mostly bright stars, about 30' across. Over 40 stars counted.
(4¼ RFT) Cluster of mainly bright stars about 30' in diameter. Not very compressed. About 30 stars seen at x42. 12 CMa is on the edge of the cluster.

Ruprecht 8	07 01.6	−13 35		4	IV 2 p	CMa

---

(10) Very faint, small and difficult. A mag. 8 and mag. 9 star lie at N. end. No other stars in the area are brighter than mag. 12. 9 stars seen at x80. Diam. about 6'.

Catalogue	R.A.	Dec.	mag.	A.D.	Type	Const.
NGC 2360	07 17.6	−15 38	9.1	14	II 2 m	CMa

(6) Rich, compact group with nebulosity of unresolved stars. A tapering arm of faint stars and nebulosity points S., ending with a brighter star.

Catalogue	R.A.	Dec.	mag.	A.D.	Type	Const.
NGC 2362	07 18.6	−24 58	3.9	6	I 3 p	CMa
	Nuc. of Vel. OB1.					

(8) A fairly large (15') group with a mag. 4 star at centre. Little concentration to centre. Loose but rich in fainter stars. 30 stars seen of mag. 9 - 11.
(4¼ RFT) Small, densely packed cluster, about 10' in diameter, surrounding τ CMa. Over 20 stars seen at x42.

Catalogue	R.A.	Dec.	mag.	A.D.	Type	Const.
NGC 2367	07 20.2	−21 56	7.8	3.5	IV 3 p	CMa

(12½) Pretty rich, wedge-shaped cluster elongated N.E.-S.W., size 10' x 5'. Stars pretty bright, 21 being counted in the magnitude range 10 - 13. No central condensation.
(6) Small cluster containing 10 distinct stars and other fainter members. The brightest stars are arranged in a Y-shape.

	R.A.	Dec.				Const.
	07 24.0	−31 50				CMa

(4¼ RFT) A large asterism of mostly bright stars spread over about 1 degree. Twelve stars seen, ranging from mag. 5 - 9, including a lovely double in the centre (Δ47). The brightest component of the double is orange, but all the other stars in the asterism are white. Reminiscent of 'Brocchi's Cluster' in Vulpecula.

Catalogue	R.A.	Dec.	mag.	A.D.	Type	Const.
NGC 2383	07 24.8	−20 56	8.8	5.5	I 3 m	CMa

(6) Small, faint cluster in a field of faint stars. Appears nebulous, but not difficult. The asterism NGC 2384 is nearby.

Catalogue	R.A.	Dec.	mag.	A.D.	Type	Const.
NGC 2421	07 36.4	−20 36	8.6	8	I 2 m	Pup

(10) A well defined, fairly rich cluster about 8' in diameter. 8 fairly bright stars and more fainter ones.

Catalogue	R.A.	Dec.	mag.	A.D.	Type	Const.
NGC 2422 M.47	07 36.6	−14 28	4.3	30	III 2 m	Pup

(8½) A striking cluster even in 6x30 finder, with a number of stars clearly seen embedded in a sparkling nebulosity. With the telescope, the cluster was noted to have a number of bright stars, including two conspicuous doubles Σ 1120 and Σ 1121. 25 stars clearly recorded.
(6) Extremely large and scattered but a rich cluster; contains numerous bright stars. Fills entire 25' field. Fine double near centre (mag. 7, 10). Little concentration towards the centre.

Catalogue	R.A.	Dec.	mag.	A.D.	Type	Const.
NGC 2437 M.46	07 41.8	−14 48	6.6	27	III 2 m	Pup

NGC 2438 is a foreground object.

(8½) Pretty cluster of mostly faint stars in a field about 30' diameter. Contains a large number of stars, densely packed, perhaps 150 or more altogether. Magnitude range of stars is comparatively small. PN NGC 2438 involved, on N. edge of cluster.

Catalogue	R.A.	Dec.	mag.	A.D.	Type	Const.
NGC 2439	07 41.0	−31 40	7.1	10	II 3 m	Pup

(4¼ RFT) Circular haze of small extent around R Puppis. 2/3 faint stars suspected within the haze.

Catalogue	R.A.	Dec.	mag.	A.D.	Type	Const.
NGC 2447 M.93	07 44.5	−23 52	6.3	23	IV 1 p	Pup

(6) A brilliant cluster with 2 v. bright stars and many stars of mag. 10 and below. Fairly concentrated and rich but very little gathered to the centre.
(4¼ RFT) A roughly wedge-shaped cluster, densely packed with faintish stars so that it appears almost nebulous. Diam. 30'.

Catalogue	R.A.	Dec.	mag.	A.D.	Type	Const.
NGC 2451	07 45.4	−37 59	3.7	45	II 2 p	Pup

(4¼ RFT) Large cluster, about 45' across, in a magnificent 3° field, containing many bright stars. The cluster is centred on a triangle of bright stars, the lucida (c Puppis) being a distinct orange colour. 15 stars seen at x16.

Catalogue	R.A.	Dec.	mag.	A.D.	Type	Const.
NGC 2453	07 47.7	−27 16	8.6	5	I 2 p	Pup

(12½) Hazy, partly resolved cluster. A wedge-shaped group of 4 mag. 8 stars plus 14 mag. 11 − 13 stars. PN NGC 2452 10' S.
(10) Circular cluster about 5' in diameter close to a mag. 9 star. Inner condensed area in which 5 stars of mag. 10 and below are seen.
(3) Faint and small; tightly grouped at centre.

Catalogue	R.A.	Dec.	mag.	A.D.	Type	Const.
Trumpler 9	07 55.2	−25 56	9.0	6	I 2 p	Pup

----

(10) An irregular cluster of about 15 stars. At high power is an inner scattering of faint stars with a heavily condensed region in the S.E. part, in which 2 stars only are visible in nebulosity of 2' diameter.

Catalogue	R.A.	Dec.	mag.	A.D.	Type	Const.
NGC 2489	07 56.2	−30 04	9.2	9	II 2 m	Pup

($4\frac{1}{4}$ RFT) Faint oval glow about 10' in diameter with two fairly faint stars superimposed. The cluster is N.f. an orange star which is the central of 3 bright stars (x16).

Catalogue	R.A.	Dec.	mag.	A.D.	Type	Const.
NGC 2516	07 58.3	−60 52	3.3	22	I 3 r	Car

----

(6) A glorious cluster of about 100 stars in a field about 40' in diameter, dominated by 3 bright orange stars. The greatest density of stars is on W. edge.
($4\frac{1}{2}$) Large and practically fills a low power field. Stars very condensed.
(12x40) Bright cluster, easily visible with the naked-eye and in binoculars is just about fully resolved into many bright stars. At least 6 pairs noted. Central region hazy with unresolved stars.

Catalogue	R.A.	Dec.	mag.	A.D.	Type	Const.
NGC 2527	08 05.2	−28 29	8.0	22	III 1 p	Pup

----

(6) Moderately rich but coarse cluster, some 20' x 15' in extent, and elongated E-W. The brightest members (mag. 9 & 10) lie near the E. edge. About half the members are fainter than mag. 11. A line of 3 mag. 8 & 9 stars, 8' long, lie 15' S.E. and aid identification.

Catalogue	R.A.	Dec.	mag.	A.D.	Type	Const.
NGC 2547	08 10.6	−49 16	5.0	25	II 2 p	Vel

(12½) Extremely large. Very rich but pretty loose, with no central condensation evident. Orientated approx. S.W.−N.E. 29 stars seen of mag. 8 − 12 plus one mag. 7 star S. of centre. (6) Large cluster about 2° away from γ Vel. Over 50 stars visible of mag. 6 and below. At the centre of the cluster the stars form a miniature 'Crux' and the eastern star of this cross appears to be double.

Catalogue	R.A.	Dec.	mag.	A.D.	Type	Const.
NGC 2660	08 42.2	−47 08	11.0	3	I 1 r	Vel

(6) A small, faint compressed cluster not resolved properly at less than x114, when it appeared slightly globular.

Catalogue	R.A.	Dec.	mag.	A.D.	Type	Const.
IC 2395	08 44.9	−48 11	4.6	17	II 3 p	Vel

(6) Loose association of about 20 stars, roughly in an egg-shape pattern.

Catalogue	R.A.	Dec.	mag.	A.D.	Type	Const.
NGC 2671	08 46.2	−41 53	11.5	3	I 3 p	Vel

(12½) Pretty rich, compact cluster, with 19 faint stars seen (mostly mag. 11 − 12). Cluster near 2 mag. 10 stars.

Catalogue	R.A.	Dec.	mag.	A.D.	Type	Const.
NGC 2818A	09 16.0	−36 36	8.2	9	II 2 m	Pyx

(12½) Coarse open cluster (about 8' x 6') of 16 stars of mag. 9 − 12. PN NGC 2818 on N. edge of cluster.

Catalogue	R.A.	Dec.	mag.	A.D.	Type	Const.
NGC 2910	09 30.4	-52 54	7.2	5	I 2 p	Vel

(6) At x114, seen to consist of 15 - 20 stars of about mag. 10 and below in a roughly horseshoe-shape. About 7' diameter.

Catalogue	R.A.	Dec.	mag.	A.D.	Type	Const.
NGC 2925	09 33.7	-53 26	8.3	12	III 1 p	Vel

(12½) Bright arc of a couple of dozen stars.

Catalogue	R.A.	Dec.	mag.	A.D.	Type	Const.
NGC 2972	09 40.3	-50 20	9.9	4	I 1 p	Vel

(12½) Small, web-like group of stars.

Catalogue	R.A.	Dec.	mag.	A.D.	Type	Const.
NGC 3033	09 48.8	-56 25	8.8	5	II 3 p	Vel

(12½) Only a few stars visible in this cluster; hard to distinguish from the background.
(6) Faint cluster of about 20 stars, some 8' across and arranged to give the impression of a figure '6'. Difficult to see at x32, best seen at x114.

Catalogue	R.A.	Dec.	mag.	A.D.	Type	Const.
NGC 3105	10 00.8	-54 46	9.7	2	I 3 p	Vel

(40) A group of 18 stars in a field 2' x 1'.

38

Catalogue	R.A.	Dec.	mag.	A.D.	Type	Const.
NGC 3114	10 02.7	−60 07	4.5	35	II 3 r	Car

(6) Very rich and very large. A beautiful cluster of over 100 stars of mag. 9 and below. Rectangular shape.
(4½) A large though loose cluster which can also be seen with the naked-eye as a small, faint 'cloud' N.p. q Carinae.

NGC 3228	10 21.7	−51 44	6.4	18	I 1 p	Vel

(6) Large, coarse and scattered group with a prominent triangle of 3 bright stars at centre. Somewhat elongated in an E-W direction. 16 stars noted.

NGC 3293	10 35.8	−58 14	6.2	6	I 3 r	Car

d = 2.6 kpc. Car OB1.

(6) Bright, rich, compressed cluster, about 8' in diameter. Contains about 50 stars of about mag. 6 and fainter. Seems globular in finder.
(4¼) Small, compact and easy cluster. 12 stars seen at x30. Angularly round.

IC 2602	10 42.7	−64 24	1.6	50	II 3 m	Car

(6) Cluster surrounding bright orange star θ Carinae. Contains about 30 stars brighter than mag. 9 and many more fainter ones.
(12x40) Large, bright cluster, several members of which can be seen with the naked-eye. About 35 stars seen using binoculars. Closely S. is the fainter cluster Mel. 101, which appears as a small elliptical spot.

Catalogue	R.A.	Dec.	mag.	A.D.	Type	Const.
NGC 3532	11 06.4	-58 40	3.4	55	II 1 m	Car

Contains several red giants.

----

(6) Very large, very bright and extremely rich! Contains
apparently hundreds of stars, mostly blue and white, but also
one bright orange star and a group of 3 fainter orange stars.
Elongated E-W. Stars arranged in lines and evenly distributed.
Brightest stars are of mag. 8.
($4\frac{1}{4}$) Extremely rich and large. Wedge-shaped, stars forming
curving lines. Elongated E-W.
(12x40) Elliptical cluster, substantially resolved into faint
stars of about mag. 8 and below. The object is broken by an
indentation on N.W. side.

NGC 3603	11 15.1	-61 15	10.5	2.5	I 1 p	Car

----

(6) Very faint nebulous spot at x32. Seems to be resolved at
x114, but still appears to have nebulosity involved.

Mel. 105	11 19.5	-63 30	9.5	5	I 2 r	Car

d = 2.1 kpc.

----

(6) At x32, seen as a tiny hazy spot of light. Partly resolved
at x114 into a nebulous cluster of slightly triangular shape.

NGC 3766	11 36.2	-61 36	4.6	15	I 1 p	Cen

----

(6) Beautiful cluster of 50 - 70 stars of mag. 8 - 13, in a
shape reminiscent of a wine glass. Some orange and yellow
stars are visible, contrasting with the remaining predominantly
white stars. Cluster about 10' diameter.

Catalogue	R.A.	Dec.	mag.	A.D.	Type	Const.
NGC 3909	11 49.6	−48 15				Cen

RNGC Class 7 object.

(12½) Very large and scattered with 34 stars of mag. 9 − 12 seen in a field 35' across. Not particularly rich.

NGC 3960	11 50.9	−55 41	9.0	7	I 2 m	Cen

(12½) Compact and very rich but faint, and only partly resolved into 15 mag. 12 stars and a background of e.f. stars.

Ruprecht 98	11 58.0	−64 29	7.0	10	II 2 p	Cru

----

(20) Loose, bright group of 40 stars in a 10' field.

NGC 4052	12 01.9	−63 12	8.8	8	II 1 p	Cru

----

(20) Rich group of 50 stars in a 12' field.
(12½) Fairly large, elongated rectangle of stars. Near δ Cru.

NGC 4103	12 06.7	−61 14	7.4	6	I 3 m	Cru

----

(20) 70 stars in a 9' field.
(12½) Pretty compact and rich. 16 stars seen of mag. 10 − 11. Impact of cluster reduced because of low altitude (approx. 4½° above horizon.

Catalogue	R.A.	Dec.	mag.	A.D.	Type	Const.
NGC 4349	12 24.5	-61 54	7.4	16	I 2 m	Cru

(20) Cluster of about 150 stars in a field 18' in diameter; the brightest is of about mag. 13. Centre strangely dark. (12½) A broad, rich cluster featuring very striking chains of stars, along with what appear to be dark lanes. It is not clear whether these are real or a contrast illusion.

Catalogue	R.A.	Dec.	mag.	A.D.	Type	Const.
NGC 4439	12 28.4	-60 06	8.4	4	II 1 p	Cru

(20) A cluster of about 20 faint stars in a 6' field. (12½) Half-moon shape of brightish stars. Very sparse.

Catalogue	R.A.	Dec.	mag.	A.D.	Type	Const.
NGC 4609	12 42.3	-62 58	6.9	5	II 1 p	Cru

(20) A straggly cluster of 30 stars in a field 8' across. (12½) Rectangle of bright stars seen against the black background of the 'Coalsack'.

Catalogue	R.A.	Dec.	mag.	A.D.	Type	Const.
NGC 4755 κ Cru	12 53.6 d = 2.34 kpc.	-60 21	5.2	10	I 3 r	Cru

(12) Beautiful cluster, especially fine for the colour contrasts among the stars. Many of the groups appear as triplets. To the N.W. a distinctive line of three has an orange star at N.E. end and a blue one to the S.W. The orange star is κ , but this did not seem to be the brightest, this being a greenish star to the N.W. of the cluster. (6) Over 20 stars visible in this smallish cluster, which has the shape of a capital 'A'. 10 stars dominate, forming the outline of the 'A' and the many fainter stars are found mostly on the W. leg. Star at apex of 'A' is the brightest. (4½) Not particularly large but forms an arrow-shaped group of perhaps 50 stars around κ Crucis. Some tints of red, blue and yellow can be picked out.

Catalogue	R.A.	Dec.	mag.	A.D.	Type	Const.
NGC 5299	13 50.5	-59 56				Cen

RNGC Class 7 object.

($12\frac{1}{2}$) Very large, scattered and pretty rich group with a mag. 7 star at E. edge. 23 stars noted of mags 9 & 10.

NGC 5460	14 07.7	-48 19	6.1	35	II 3 m	Cen

----

(6) Scattered cluster, easily resolved into bright stars and elongated roughly N-S. Cluster includes a concentrated knot of 7 stars at mid-point. 22 stars counted of mag. 8 - 11.

NGC 5823	15 05.7	-55 36	8.6	12	III 2 m	Cir

($12\frac{1}{2}$) Pretty rich, large, round group, including 4 mag. 10 stars at W. and S. side. Stars evenly distributed overall with a small bright Y-shaped asterism. 30 stars noted of mag. 10 - 12.

NGC 5999	15 52.2	-56 29	9.0	4	I 3 m	Nor

($12\frac{1}{2}$) Small, compact and rich. The cluster has an arrowhead shape and includes 4 mag. 11 stars and at least 30 of mag. 12 to 13.
(6) Concentrated cluster, resolves quite well at x114. About 100 stars estimated visible.

NGC 6025	16 03.6	-60 30	6.0	15	II 2 p	TrA

($2\frac{1}{4}$ O.G.) Bright cluster of about 20 stars of mag. 7 and below. Not large but pretty, with stars flowing in streamers.

Catalogue	R.A.	Dec.	mag.	A.D.	Type	Const.
NGC 6152	16 32.7	−52 37	7.7	30	II 2 m	Nor

(10) Large, coarse, bright and pretty rich cluster; little compressed but includes a small, 3' diameter, knot of 8 stars W. Stars seem aligned in strings. In a 20' field, 37 stars seen of mag. 9 - 11.

| NGC 6193 | 16 41.4 | −48 46 | 5.4 | 15 | II 3 p | Ara |

(6) Pretty cluster of stars like fine sand, resolved at x73. Cluster slightly heart-shaped. Double star h 4876 lies in the southern part of the cluster, possibly resolved at x230.

| NGC 6204 | 16 46.5 | −47 02 | 8.4 | 6 | I 3 m | Ara |

(10) Compact, rich cluster of fairly faint stars, including several nice doubles. 28 stars noted of mag. 9 - 12, with a mag. 9 star at centre. A line of 5 stars extends S.S.E.

| NGC 6231 | 16 54.2 | −41 48 | 3.4 | 15 | I 3 p | Sco |

Sco OB1. Contains W-R stars.

(6) A brilliant cluster with a group of 7/8 particularly bright stars at the centre, which gives the impression of a cluster within a cluster. Possibly over 100 stars visible altogether. (4¼) Large, brilliant cluster. 17 stars counted to about mag. 10 with a background of extremely faint members. (4¼ RFT) Small cluster of intense white stars in a very rich field, including nearby ζ^1 and ζ^2 Sco. About 10 stars seen at x16.

Catalogue	R.A.	Dec.	mag.	A.D.	Type	Const.
NGC 6242	16 55.6	-39 30	8.2	9	I 3 m	Sco
	Sco OB1.					

(4¼ RFT) Small, poorly resolved object at x16. Fan-shaped, with comparatively bright star at apex.

| Trumpler 24 | 16 56.2 | -40 43 | 8.5 | 40 | IV 2 p | Sco |
| H. 12 | Sco OB1. Faint H II region IC 4628 associated. | | | | | |

(6) Very large cluster with streams of stars in all directions. (4¼ RFT) A very large object, about 2° across. Rather thinly populated and with no distinct structure. Includes 16 stars of mag. 10 or brighter.

| NGC 6268 | 17 02.1 | -39 43 | 9.5 | 10 | II 2 p | Sco |
| | Sco OB1. | | | | | |

(10) Compact, rich, bright group with stars arranged in three prominent lines. The cluster has a roughly triangular outline and includes one very close double. 45 stars seen of mag. 10 to 13.

| NGC 6281 | 17 04.8 | -37 53 | 8.5 | 9 | II 2 p | Sco |

(6) Conspicuous arrow-shaped cluster with a half-circle of stars just S.

Catalogue	R.A.	Dec.	mag.	A.D.	Type	Const.
NGC 6322	17 18.5	−42 58	6.5	10	I 2 p	Sco

(10) Small, compact and rich. A bright triangular cluster with 3 mag. 9 stars at the corners and 30 others of about mag. 10 – 12. Stars evenly distributed.
(4¼ RFT) A small cluster, about 15' across, with a distinct triangle of stars forming its outline; these are of approx. equal magnitude and equidistant. Near the southernmost of the stars, and enclosed within the triangle, is a small group of perhaps 3/4 tiny stars, difficult to resolve. 2 other faintish stars close by.

Catalogue	R.A.	Dec.	mag.	A.D.	Type	Const.
NGC 6383	17 34.6	−32 35	5.4	20	IV 3 p	Sco

includes V 701 Sco (eclipsing binary).

(10) Fairly compact and rich group with a fine multiple star, with yellow primary, at centre. Stars, mostly in lines, extend N. and S. 19 stars of mag. 10 – 12 visible.

Catalogue	R.A.	Dec.	mag.	A.D.	Type	Const.
IC 4651	17 24.6	−49 57	7.8	10	II 2 r	Ara

(6) A lovely cluster of seemingly hundreds of stars. Stars mostly faint.

Catalogue	R.A.	Dec.	mag.	A.D.	Type	Const.
NGC 6405 M.6	17 40.0	−32 12	5.3	20	III 2 p	Sco

incl. BM Sco., 6.0 – 8.1, p. 850d. & V 862 Sco.

(4¼) Large and bright; resembles a butterfly. 35 stars noted. Pretty rich but without any evident concentration toward the centre. Elongated E.N.E.–W.S.W.
(4¼ RFT) At x16, 20 stars seen in a field about 30' across, though many more detected on limit of resolution. All stars white except one, which is orange (BM Sco.).

Catalogue	R.A.	Dec.	mag.	A.D.	Type	Const.
NGC 6475 M.7	17 54.0	−34 49	4.1	80	II 2 r	Sco

(6) A very rich, large and bright group! Includes 2 fine
doubles of equal mags. Prominent geometric shapes evident.
Stars seem to be either very bright or very faint.
($4\frac{1}{4}$ RFT) A magnificent cluster! At x16, the entire $3°$ field
is filled with brilliant white stars, though the main area of
the cluster seems to be about $1°.5$ in diameter. About 30
stars visible altogether, centred on a bright double. Cluster
projected against a luminous Milky Way background.

NGC 6520	18 03.5	−27 54	7.6	5	I 2 m	Sgr

Dark nebula B.86 adjacent.

(10) Small, compact, rich cluster on the edge of a prominent
dark nebula. The cluster contains 6 mag. 7/8 stars plus many
fainter stars of about mag. 10.

NGC 6531 M.21	18 04.7	−22 30	6.7	15	I 3 m	Sgr

($4\frac{1}{4}$) Large, scattered, loose group of 25 stars of mag. 9 − 11.
No concentration evident.
($4\frac{1}{4}$ RFT) Smallish cluster not far from the nebula NGC 6514
(M.20) and seemingly joined to it by a string of stars.
Cluster resolved clearly into about half a dozen stars at x16,
and near the brightest of these is an almost nebulous haze of
fainter stars.

NGC 6540	18 06.4	−27 49		0.5	III 1 p	Sgr

(6) Very faint cluster, visible as just a diffuse spot.

Catalogue	R.A.	Dec.	mag.	A.D.	Type	Const.
NGC 6568	18 12.8	−21 36	8.4	13	III 1 m	Sgr

(8) Rather faint and open with few bright stars; an S-shaped curve in the centre surrounded by a fine clustering of faint members. 14 Sgr. lies 20' E.

Trumpler 32	18 17.5	−13 20	12.2	4	I 2 m	Ser

(10) Very faint, small and difficult. The brightest star is of mag. 12 and x120 is needed to resolve the few members visible. Evidence of a very rich object requiring a large aperture. About 3' diam.

NGC 6611	18 18.8	−13 47	6.5	8	II 3 m	Ser
M. 16	Nebulosity involved.		d = 2.5 kpc.	Ser OB1.		

(8½) Striking cluster about 20' in diameter, containing a large number of stars. Quite a few of the stars are bright with a tremendous number of faint stars intermingled, particularly at N. side. Slight trace of nebulosity suspected around the wide double which is formed by 2 of the brightest stars of the cluster.
(8) Rich cluster surrounding large nebulous patch of indefinite shape. Cluster very spread out and large.

NGC 6613	18 19.9	−17 08	8.5	10	II 3 p	Sgr
M. 18						

(8½) Smallish cluster, about 10' in diameter, with fairly bright stars of about mag. 9 - 10. All the stars are white, with some doubles. Cluster adjacent to a mag. 6 star easily located in finder.

Catalogue	R.A.	Dec.	mag.	A.D.	Type	Const.
IC 4725	18 31.7	−19 15	6.5	33	I 2 p	Sgr
M.25	Includes Cepheid U Sgr., p = 6.75d.					

(8½) Coarse cluster of about 18 stars, some 20' in diameter. Most stars concentrated in N. part of cluster. All the stars appear white except the brightest, which is orange (U Sgr).

NGC 6645	18 32.6	−16 54	8.3	11	III 1 m	Sgr

(8) A cloud of very faint stars including a fairly bright triple. The cluster contains about 60 stars in a roundish shape, over ¾ being of about mag. 12; mag. 11/11.5 outliers extend in all directions comprising about 30 to 40 additional stars. Main body 6' diameter, outliers extend this to 10'.

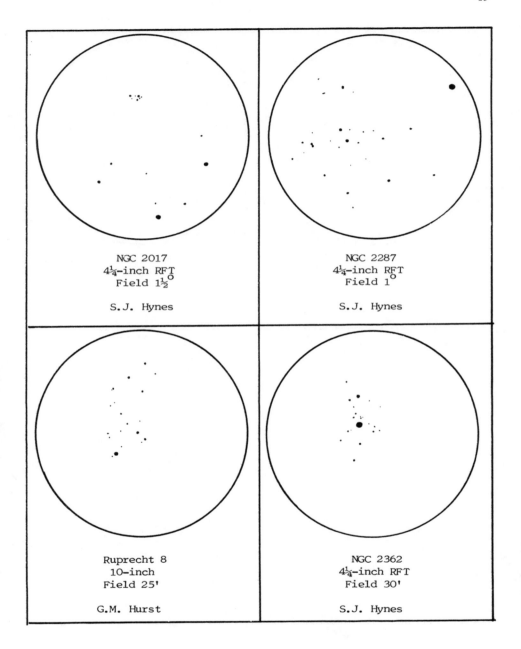

NGC 2017
4¼-inch RFT
Field 1½°

S.J. Hynes

NGC 2287
4¼-inch RFT
Field 1°

S.J. Hynes

Ruprecht 8
10-inch
Field 25'

G.M. Hurst

NGC 2362
4¼-inch RFT
Field 30'

S.J. Hynes

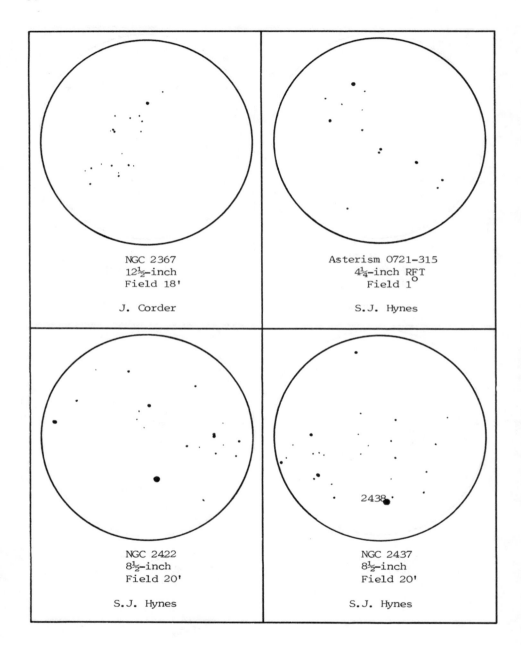

NGC 2367
12½-inch
Field 18'

J. Corder

Asterism 0721-315
4¼-inch RFT
Field 1°

S.J. Hynes

NGC 2422
8½-inch
Field 20'

S.J. Hynes

NGC 2437
8½-inch
Field 20'

S.J. Hynes

2438

51

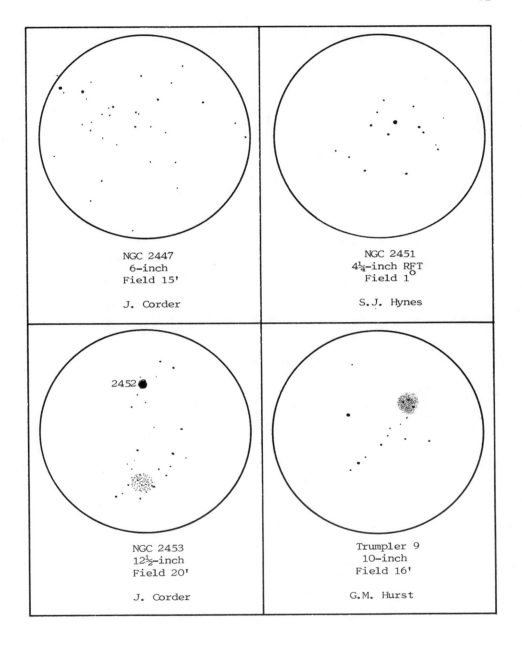

NGC 2447
6-inch
Field 15'

J. Corder

NGC 2451
4¼-inch RFT
Field 1°

S.J. Hynes

2452

NGC 2453
12½-inch
Field 20'

J. Corder

Trumpler 9
10-inch
Field 16'

G.M. Hurst

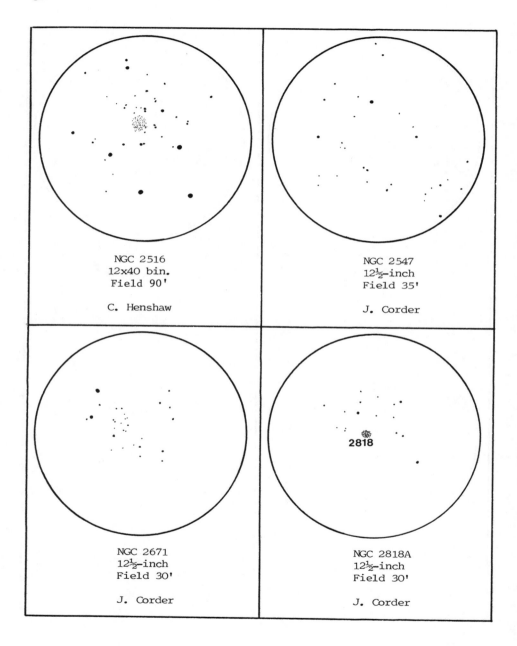

NGC 2516
12x40 bin.
Field 90'

C. Henshaw

NGC 2547
12½-inch
Field 35'

J. Corder

NGC 2671
12½-inch
Field 30'

J. Corder

2818

NGC 2818A
12½-inch
Field 30'

J. Corder

53

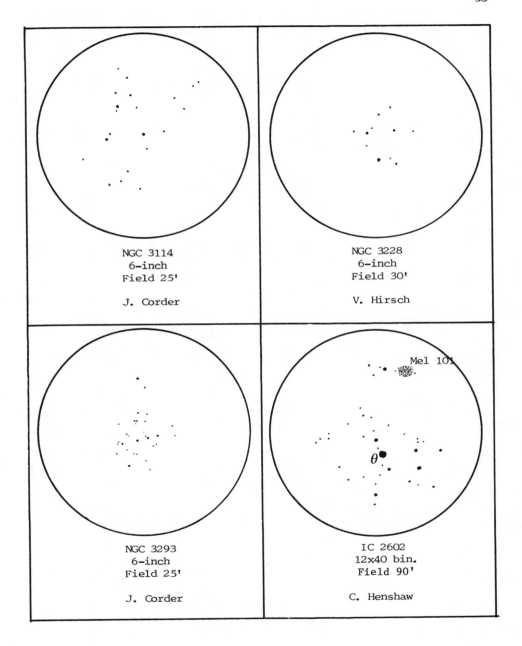

NGC 3114
6-inch
Field 25'

J. Corder

NGC 3228
6-inch
Field 30'

V. Hirsch

NGC 3293
6-inch
Field 25'

J. Corder

Mel 101

θ

IC 2602
12x40 bin.
Field 90'

C. Henshaw

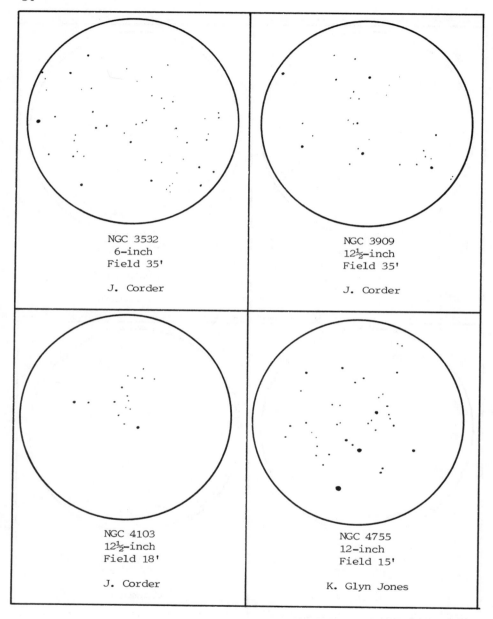

NGC 3532
6-inch
Field 35'

J. Corder

NGC 3909
12½-inch
Field 35'

J. Corder

NGC 4103
12½-inch
Field 18'

J. Corder

NGC 4755
12-inch
Field 15'

K. Glyn Jones

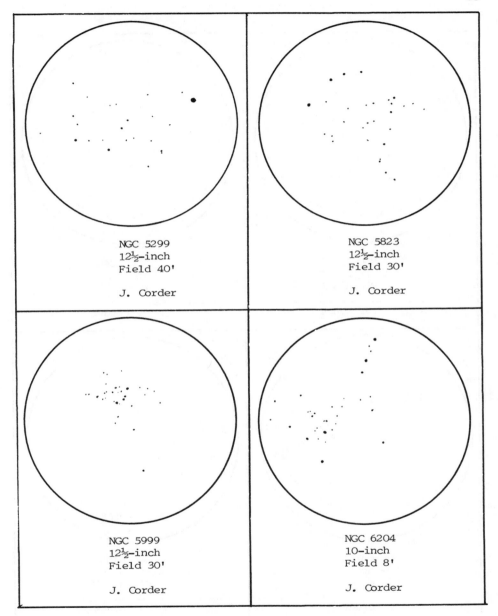

NGC 5299
12½-inch
Field 40'

J. Corder

NGC 5823
12½-inch
Field 30'

J. Corder

NGC 5999
12½-inch
Field 30'

J. Corder

NGC 6204
10-inch
Field 8'

J. Corder

56

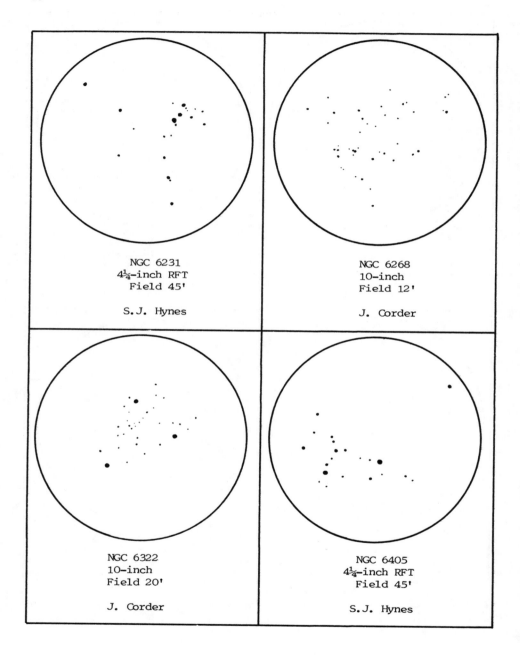

NGC 6231
4¼-inch RFT
Field 45'

S.J. Hynes

NGC 6268
10-inch
Field 12'

J. Corder

NGC 6322
10-inch
Field 20'

J. Corder

NGC 6405
4¼-inch RFT
Field 45'

S.J. Hynes

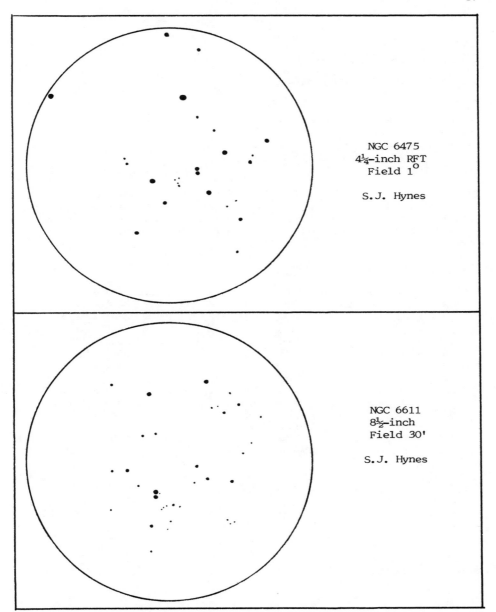

NGC 6475
4¼-inch RFT
Field 1°

S.J. Hynes

NGC 6611
8½-inch
Field 30'

S.J. Hynes

Catalogue

SECTION 2: GLOBULAR CLUSTERS

Data provided with this section:

(a) Catalogue number
(b) R.A. and Dec. for Epoch 2000.0
(c) Apparent magnitude
(d) Spectral type
(e) Concentration class
(f) Constellation

The data in (c) and (d) is taken from the Astronomical Almanac 1984, page H.54 and is based on a list supplied by Dr. Helen Sawyer Hogg. The data in (e) is taken from Atlas Coeli (Becvar, 1964). In a number of cases additional information will be found on the line below the basic data.

Observers and Accredited Objects

NGC		NGC		NGC	
104	RJB, VH	6121	JC, SS, CN, SJH	6441	VH
288	JC, RJM, VH	6139	VH	6496	JC
362	VH	6144	MJT, VH	6541	JC
1049	JC	6171	CN, JC	6544	VH
1261	VH	6235	MJT, SS, VH	6553	VH
1851	JC	6266	JC, KGJ	6584	JC
1904	KGJ	6273	KGJ	6624	JC
2298	MJT, JC, VH	6284	VH	6626	CN, SJH
2808	VH	6287	VH	6637	KGJ, JC
3201	JC, VH	6293	VH	6638	GH, VH
4590	JC	6316	VH	6642	MJT
4833	VH	6333	JC	6652	JC
5139	MJT, VH, CF	6342	JP	6656	JC, GH, SJH
5286	JC, VH	6352	VH	6681	KGJ, JC
5824	SS	6355	VH	6715	CN
5897	MJT, JC	6356	JP	6723	JC, VH, SJH
5927	VH	6362	RJB, VH	6752	VH
5946	VH	6380	JC	6809	JC
5986	VH	6388	JC, VH	6864	DAA, KGJ
6093	CN, JC	6397	JC, VH	6981	MJT
6101	RJE	6440	MJT	7099	CN, JC

59

Catalogue	R.A.	Dec.	mag.	Type	Con. cl.	Const.
NGC 104	00 24.1	−72 04	4.0	G	III	Tuc
47 Tuc.	30 known variables. Xr.					

(36) Beautiful globular filling the entire field of view at
x500. Certainly over 3000 stars must be visible. The cluster
looks 3-dimensional.
(6) Near SMC. A smaller version of omega Cen. Has a very
bright nucleus and resolves into hundreds of stars with many
outliers.

NGC 288	00 52.6	−26 36	8.1	F	X	Scl

(12½) Very large and very bright. Coarse and well resolved
out to about 8.' diameter with a core about 5' in size. The
brightest stars seem to be about mag. 11.5. Prominent string
of stars to S.
(8) An irregularly round nebulous glow about 10' across with
perhaps a dozen stars resolved.
(6) Fairly large and of low surface brightness. Faint
concentration of mag. 12 stars seen at x114.
(2¼) Nearly round and of even brightness. Fairly large.

NGC 362	01 02.3	−70 51	6.6	F	III	Tuc

(6) Has a bright nucleus but does not resolve. Lies in a
barren field.

NGC 1049	02 39.8	−34 17	13.0		V	For

GCl. in Fornax dwarf elliptical galaxy. Two other globulars
are also present, one 35' away in P.A. 203°, the other 17'
distant in P.A. 165° (mag. 8 star 7' p.).

(12½) Extremely faint and difficult. Fairly large (diam. 50'')
and round with no central brightening. 2nd globular also seen.

Catalogue	R.A.	Dec.	mag.	Type	Con. cl.	Const.
NGC 1261	03 12.3	-55 13	8.4	F	II	Hor

(6) Faint but large. Slightly brighter central region.

NGC 1851	05 14.0	-40 01	7.3	F		Col

Xrb (=4U 0513-40).

($12\frac{1}{2}$) Very bright. Round, and contains a very much brighter
round nucleus. One mag. 12 star and many very faint member
stars resolved, but on N.W. side only.
(6) Bright, fine object, but not even slightly resolved.
Gradually brightens to the centre. Round.

NGC 1904	05 24.3	-24 31	7.8	F	V	Lep
M.79						

(8) Small object. Outer areas resolved at x241, more so to
the N.

NGC 2298	06 48.9	-36 01	9.4	F	VI	Pup

($16\frac{1}{2}$) Small object, brightening towards the centre. The outer
edges are resolved at x176 and considerably more stars are
seen at x351. Somewhat irregular in shape.
(8) Pretty faint, round and of even surface brightness. Seems
mottled with some resolution of N. edge.
(6) Faint, slightly brightening towards centre. No sign of
resolution.

Catalogue	R.A.	Dec.	mag.	Type	Con. cl.	Const.
NGC 2808	09 11.8	−64 51	6.3	F	I	Car

(6) A prominent object in a sparse field. About 5' diameter.
Many faint stars on limit of resolution, a few outlying stars
more clearly seen.

NGC 3201	10 17.5	−46 25	6.7	F	X	Vel

92 known variables.

(12½) Very large, bright globular of roughly triangular shape.
Not very compressed, brighter stars stand out well against a
mottled background. Star distribution very uneven; 2 knots
noted (S.p. and S.f.), both elongated. About 50 stars of mag.
12 - 14 seen with direct vision.
(6) Large, faint globular, with some stars resolved at x230.
There appears to be a greater concentration of stars in a
crescent-shape across the northern side of the cluster, fading
away towards the S.

NGC 4590	12 39.5	−26 45	8.5	F	X	Hya
M.68						

42 known variables.

(8) Bright, round and pretty large. Very mottled and of
granular appearance. No central brightening, about 12 - 15
e.f. members resolved.

NGC 4833	12 59.4	−70 52	7.3	F	VIII	Mus

(6) Large and very faint luminous patch. No trace of
resolution. Mag. 9 star due N. interferes with observation.

Catalogue	R.A.	Dec.	mag.	Type	Con. cl.	Const.
NGC 5139	13 26.8	−47 29	3.6	F	VIII	Cen
ωCen.	200 known variables.					

($16\frac{1}{2}$) An awesome sight. So large and easily resolved that the 3-dimensional effect is unbelievable. Countless stars fill the entire field of view, the entire cluster being resolved right through the central region.
(6) Easily resolved into a large number of stars, some forming streams. Very bright central region.
($4\frac{1}{2}$) Resolved into stars at the edges even at x50. About $\frac{1}{2}^{\circ}$ in diameter.

NGC 5286	13 46.1	−51 23	7.6	F	V	Cen

----

(6) Large globular in a beautiful field. Concentrated, bright nucleus with filaments of stars trailing off to the sides. Bright star to the S.

NGC 5824	15 03.9	−33 05	9.0	F	I	Lup
	27 known variables.					

----

(10) At x59, fairly large and bright with a slightly brighter centre. Slightly resolved at x296 with a halo of fainter stars around the main body.

NGC 5897	15 17.3	−21 00	8.5	F	XI	Lib

($16\frac{1}{2}$) Large but not bright and only slightly brighter in the centre. Many faint stars visible at x70. Cluster lacks a highly concentrated centre and any bright members.
(8) Large and dim with an even surface brightness. Round. No resolution. Series of stars in field immediately N.

Catalogue	R.A.	Dec.	mag.	Type	Con. cl.	Const.
NGC 5927	15 28.0	−50 39	8.3	G	VIII	Lup

(6) Large globular in a fine field. Not very bright; evenly lit. Edges seem ragged.

Catalogue	R.A.	Dec.	mag.	Type	Con. cl.	Const.
NGC 5946	15 35.4	−50 40	9.6	F	IX	Nor

(6) Tiny, faint object in a fine field. Has a brighter nucleus which seemed double, like two small stars side by side.

Catalogue	R.A.	Dec.	mag.	Type	Con. cl.	Const.
NGC 5986	15 46.1	−37 47	7.1	F	VII	Lup

(6) Round, hazy object with a bright nucleus. Some outlying stars resolved.

Catalogue	R.A.	Dec.	mag.	Type	Con. cl.	Const.
NGC 6093 M.80	16 17.1	−22 59	7.2	F	II	Sco

Nova (mag. 6.5) seen in 1860.

($8\frac{1}{2}$) Small and condensed towards the centre. Granularity suspected at x155.
(8) Very bright with an extremely bright nucleus. Round. No resolution at x100.

Catalogue	R.A.	Dec.	mag.	Type	Con. cl.	Const.
NGC 6101	16 25.5	−72 12	9.3	F	X	Aps

(40) At x 200 the object is barely recognizable as a globular cluster. Many stars resolved.

64

Catalogue	R.A.	Dec.	mag.	Type	Con. cl.	Const.
NGC 6121 M.4	16 23.7 46 known variables.	−26 31	5.9	F	IX	Sco

(10) At x59, quite large and bright. Well resolved, appearing
very scattered, though more compact towards the centre. At
the very centre is an almost straight line of very bright
stars running S.p.–N.f. Including outliers, the cluster fills
the entire field of view at x148.
(8½) Faint, although fairly well resolved. The brighter
central part appeared at times to be elongated N–S, an effect
which was better seen at x56 than x111.
(4¼ RFT) A large, ill-defined circular nebula at x16. No
distinct nucleus though gradually brighter towards the centre.
No trace of resolution.

| NGC 6139 | 16 27.7 | −38 50 | 9.2 | F | II | Sco |

(6) Small, concentrated globular with quite a distinct central
brightening.

| NGC 6144 | 16 27.3 | −26 03 | 9.1 | G | XI | Sco |

(16½) Not bright but fairly large. Only a few stars resolved,
although the background appears mottled. A bright star is
visible on N.p. edge.
(6) Large though faint smudge just N. of 2 stars which point
to it. It is necessary to ensure that nearby Antares is out
of the field in order to observe this object.

| NGC 6171
M.107 | 16h 32.5
25 known variables. | −13 03 | 8.1 | G | X | Oph |

(8½) At x56 seen as a small, faint patch of nebulosity set in
the middle of a kite-shaped group of 5 faint stars. No
resolution and no definite central brightening.
(6) Large and bright with no nucleus. Has a slightly oblong
shape. Some stars seen on N. edge but otherwise of even
surface brightness.

Catalogue	R.A.	Dec.	mag.	Type	Con. cl.	Const.
NGC 6235	16 53.5	−22 09	10.1	F	IV	Oph

(16½) Small but pretty bright. No stars resolved at x70.
(10) Some faint stars visible at x148. A number of darker
areas seen within the cluster as also is a slightly brighter
star, p. the central area.
(6) A difficult object. So faint and small that it is at the
edge of visibility. No detail apparent.

| NGC 6266 | 17 02.1 | −30 43 | 6.5 | F | IV | Oph |
| M.62 | 89 known variables. | | | | | |

(12½) Large, bright, round or slightly oblong, with a
prominent nucleus off-centred to the S.E. by about 30". Mostly
resolved around the edges, especially to W. and S., where the
brighter stars appear, and to N.E. where the most faint stars
appear and where they extend furthest from the centre.
(8) Small, very bright with a slight bluish glow. Most
condensed portion to S.E. of centre with stars fanning out to
N.W., giving a comet-like look. Moderate magnification
resolves all but S.E. part.
(6) Pretty well resolved, especially around the edges.
Slightly oblate (about 4' x 3'.5). Has a small core which is
much brighter. Some resolution across the core. Several
bright stars in the field.

| NGC 6273 | 17 02.6 | −26 15 | 6.8 | F | VIII | Oph |
| M.19 | | | | | | |

(8) Elongated slightly N-S. Edges fairly easily resolved at
M.P. At x241 very well resolved with edges quite straggling.

| NGC 6284 | 17 04.6 | −24 45 | 8.9 | F | IX | Oph |

(6) A small, compact globular, appearing almost stellar at
x32. Better seen at x115 but not resolved.

66

Catalogue	R.A.	Dec.	mag.	Type	Con. cl.	Const.
NGC 6287	17 05.2	−22 42	9.2	G	VII	Oph

(6) Fairly small, faintish object in a sparse field. A mag. 10 star to the west of the globular is slightly orange in colour.

| NGC 6293 | 17 10.3 | −26 34 | 8.2 | F | IV | Oph |

(6) Fairly bright and large globular in a field of faint stars. Brighter nucleus. Not resolved.

| NGC 6316 | 17 16.6 | −28 09 | 9.0 | G | III | Oph |

(6) Very small globular appearing almost stellar at x32 and lying almost due S. of a star slightly brighter than itself. More distinctly seen at x115 but not resolved.

| NGC 6333 M.9 | 17 19.1 | −18 31 | 7.9 | F | VIII | Oph |

(8) Pretty small and very slightly oblate. No nucleus seen. Even surface brightness. Only 5 stars resolved, on W. edge.

| NGC 6342 | 17 21.2 | −19 35 | 9.9 | G | IV | Oph |

(10) Very faint indeed. An extremely small, faint smudge of light. View not improved at higher magnifications.

Catalogue	R.A.	Dec.	mag.	Type	Con. cl.	Const.
NGC 6352	17 25.4	−48 28	6.5	G	XI	Ara

(6) Faint but quite extended globular. Not resolved.

Catalogue	R.A.	Dec.	mag.	Type	Con. cl.	Const.
NGC 6355	17 24.4	−26 20	9.6	F		Oph

(6) Very faint but quite large hazy spot, with a slightly brighter nucleus. Not resolved.

Catalogue	R.A.	Dec.	mag.	Type	Con. cl.	Const.
NGC 6356	17 23.6	−17 49	8.4	G	II	Oph

(10) Low powers show a brightening of the middle and a slight mottling of the outer edges. Higher powers reveal slight resolution and a very compact core.

Catalogue	R.A.	Dec.	mag.	Type	Con. cl.	Const.
NGC 6362	17 31.7	−67 03	8.3	F	X	Ara

(40) At x200 the cluster is very large, bright and completely resolved. Not much central condensation.
(6) Faint extended object, no detail seen.

Catalogue	R.A.	Dec.	mag.	Type	Con. cl.	Const.
NGC 6380 Ton 1	17 35.4	−39 04				Sco

(10) Small and extremely faint, with a mag. 9 star attached to S. edge. Irregularly round with very diffuse edges.

Catalogue	R.A.	Dec.	mag.	Type	Con. cl.	Const.
NGC 6388	17 36.3	−44 45	6.8	G	III	Sco

(12½) Small and very bright. Round in shape. No brighter centre. Some stars nearby, 2 very bright.
(6) Bright but not resolved even at x285. Has a brighter nucleus which appears slightly off-centre, towards the N.W.

| NGC 6397 | 17 40.9 | −53 41 | 5.6 | F | IX | Ara |

Nearest globular cluster.

(10) Very bright. Small and roughly triangular in shape. Very mottled and fairly well resolved. A prominent line of 8 stars plainly resolved on E. edge, with about 2 dozen others overall.
(6) Magnificent cluster, clearly resolved at only x100, streams of stars emanating from a bright concentrated centre. Seems slightly triangular in shape.

| NGC 6440 | 17 48.9 | −20 21 | 9.6 | G | V | Sgr |

Xr.

(16½) Small, with a bright central core surrounded by a halo of soft nebulosity. The core is almost stellar. No resolution obtained up to x222.

| NGC 6441 | 17 50.2 | −37 03 | 7.4 | G | III | Sco |

Xrb (= 4U 1746-37).

(6) Large, fine globular of generally even brightness, but brightening gradually to a small nucleus. Not resolved. G Sco. (mag. 3.5) lies 4'.5 W.

Catalogue	R.A.	Dec.	mag.	Type	Con. cl.	Const.
NGC 6496	17 59.1	−44 13	9.2	G	XII	Sco

(8) Very faint, small and of even surface brightness. Round.

Catalogue	R.A.	Dec.	mag.	Type	Con. cl.	Const.
NGC 6541	18 08.0	−43 44	6.6	F	III	CrA

(12½) Very bright. Oblate (about 6' x 5') with a much brighter round core. Well resolved to N. but only barely resolved to S. Prominent double S.E.
(8) Bright and large. V. slightly brighter in the middle.

Catalogue	R.A.	Dec.	mag.	Type	Con. cl.	Const.
NGC 6544	18 07.4	−25 01	8.2	F	IX	Sgr

(6) Small, faint and unresolved. Seen in the same low power (x32) field as NGC 6553.

Catalogue	R.A.	Dec.	mag.	Type	Con. cl.	Const.
NGC 6553	18 09.5	−25 56	8.2	G	XI	Sgr

(6) Small, faint and unresolved, a twin of NGC 6544, seen in the same low power (x32) field.

Catalogue	R.A.	Dec.	mag.	Type	Con. cl.	Const.
NGC 6584	18 18.6	−52 12	9.2	F	VIII	Tel

48 known variables.

(10) Bright and pretty small. Round. Of generally even surface brightness but mottled, with some edge resolution, the brightest stars being of about mag. 14–15. About 30–40 stars visible.

Catalogue	R.A.	Dec.	mag.	Type	Con. cl.	Const.
NGC 6624	18 23.7	−30 21	8.3	G	VI	Sgr

Xrb (= Sgr XR−4).

($4\frac{1}{4}$) Small, round and fairly bright. Very slightly brighter centre.

Catalogue	R.A.	Dec.	mag.	Type	Con. cl.	Const.
NGC 6626 M.28	18 24.6	−24 52	6.9	F	IV	Sgr

($8\frac{1}{2}$) Small, circular nebulosity, condensed towards the centre. No positive resolution at x56 or x111.
($4\frac{1}{4}$RFT) Circular (about 10' diam.), gradually brighter towards the centre. Boundary ill-defined. No trace of resolution.

Catalogue	R.A.	Dec.	mag.	Type	Con. cl.	Const.
NGC 6637 M.69	18 31.4	−32 21	7.8	G	V	Sgr

----

(8) Fairly bright but small globular. Little evidence of any central condensation. At x250 the cluster breaks up into many faint stars. A mag. 9 star lies about 8' N.W.
($4\frac{1}{4}$) Small round and bright, with a brighter core.

Catalogue	R.A.	Dec.	mag.	Type	Con. cl.	Const.
NGC 6638	18 31.0	−25 30	9.2	G	VI	Sgr

45 known variables.

----

(10) Small, moderately bright globular consisting of a bright, dense centre surrounded by a fainter halo. Not resolved.
(6) Tiny, faint amorphous glow. No sign of resolution.

Catalogue	R.A.	Dec.	mag.	Type	Con. cl.	Const.
NGC 6642	18 31.8	−23 59		G	V	Sgr

(16½) Small but quite bright, with a brighter core. A few stars resolved, especially on S. edge, at x176. More resolution obtained at x315.

NGC 6652	18 35.7	−33 00	8.9	G	VI	Sgr

(12½) Small and not very bright, no nucleus detected. Oblate in shape. One bright star seen on E. edge.

NGC 6656 M.22	18 36.4	−23 54	5.1	F	VII	Sgr

32 known variables.

(12½) Very large and bright, with a very unique form and outline. The entire 30' field (x300) is filled with cluster members, with a 'handprint' shape very prominent – the 'fingers' point S.W. Bright detached V-shape area at E. edge, with another just S. Large core (5'), well resolved.
(10) Partly resolved into myriads of stars, condensed onto a haze at centre. Stars scattered at the edges and a bright star of mag. 10–11 seen at f. edge.
(6) Large and very bright. Evenly bright overall with no apparent core. Only partly resolved. Slightly oblate in shape, size about 20' x 18'.
(4¼ RFT) Large bright globular of almost uniform brightness. Diameter about 20'. Slight granularity suspected even at x16. 3° field includes a bright orange star.

NGC 6681 M.70	18 43.3	−32 18	8.2	F	V	Sgr

(8) Small, with a sharp central condensation, around which is a fainter area. Seemingly slightly flattened to the E. Outer edges resolved at x250.

72

Catalogue	R.A.	Dec.	mag.	Type	Con. cl.	Const.
NGC 6715 M.54	18 55.2	−30 28	7.7	F	III	Sgr

80 known variables.

($8\frac{1}{2}$) Small, appearing almost as a hazy star at low powers. Centre very bright. Definitely granular at x111.

NGC 6723	18 59.6	−36 38	7.3	G	VII	Sgr

31 known variables.

($12\frac{1}{2}$) Large and bright and of even surface brightness. Much resolved, including one rather brighter star (mag. 13) N.W. of centre. No core noted. Slightly oblate.
(6) Large, bright oval patch of nebulosity. Suspected resolved at x115.
($4\frac{1}{4}$ RFT) Well defined object about 10' in diameter, with a brighter centre. No evidence of any resolution. 3° field also includes the NGC 6726-7-9 nebula complex (in CrA.).

NGC 6752	19 10.8	−60 00	5.4	F	VI	Pav

(6) Beautiful globular with streamers of stars emerging from the nucleus, the overall shape reminiscent of a spider or beetle. The cluster is resolved quite well even at x73 and with ease at x114.

NGC 6809 M.55	19 40.1	−30 56	6.9	F	XI	Sgr

($8\frac{1}{2}$) Large, resolvable with medium power. Using HP it is elongated N-S, with an irregular outline. Stars of mag. 12 and below.
(6) Large and bright with a small, very bright, round core. Some resolution noted with about 2 dozen stars seen well, especially on S.W. edge. Size about 15' x 13'.

Catalogue	R.A.	Dec.	mag.	Type	Con. cl.	Const.
NGC 6864 M.75	20 06.1	−21 55	8.5	F	I	Sgr

(12) Bright but unresolved at x80; size about 2'.
(8) About 2' − 3' in diameter with a bright centre about 1'
across. Slight mottling seen at x120.

| NGC 6981 M.72 | 20 53.5 | −12 32 | 9.3 | F | IX | Aqr |

40 known variables.

(16½) Outer edges easily resolved at x70; at x160 and x222 an
area of resolved stars on N.E. side seems almost separated by
a dark region.

| NGC 7099 M.30 | 21 40.3 | −23 11 | 7.5 | F | V | Cap |

(8½) Partially resolved at x111, especially with a.v. A line
of resolved stars extends to the N. from the cluster centre.
(6) Oblate, fairly large, bright with a brighter core. Some
resolution, around edges especially. About 3 dozen stars
seen.

74

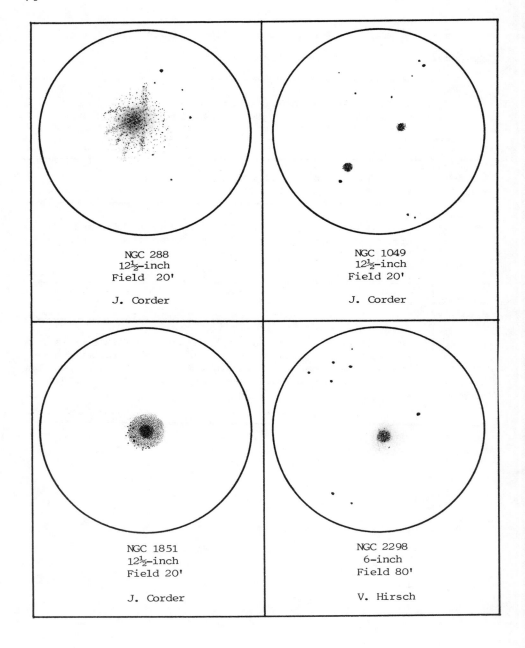

NGC 288
12½-inch
Field 20'

J. Corder

NGC 1049
12½-inch
Field 20'

J. Corder

NGC 1851
12½-inch
Field 20'

J. Corder

NGC 2298
6-inch
Field 80'

V. Hirsch

75

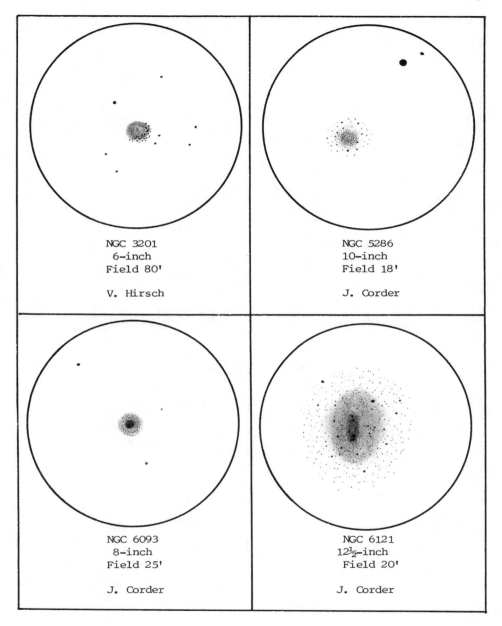

NGC 3201
6-inch
Field 80'

V. Hirsch

NGC 5286
10-inch
Field 18'

J. Corder

NGC 6093
8-inch
Field 25'

J. Corder

NGC 6121
12½-inch
Field 20'

J. Corder

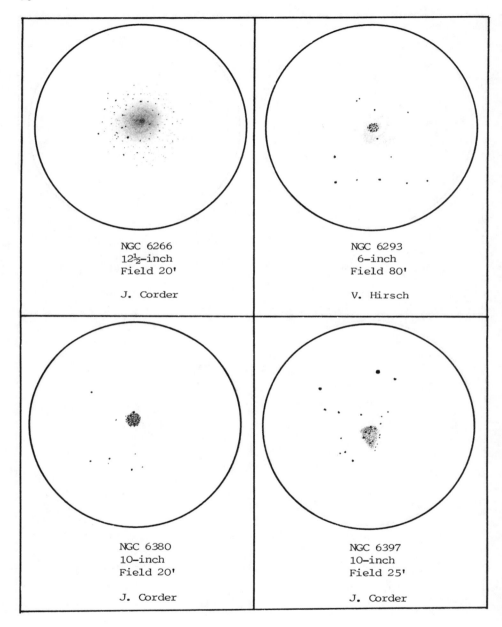

NGC 6266
12½-inch
Field 20'

J. Corder

NGC 6293
6-inch
Field 80'

V. Hirsch

NGC 6380
10-inch
Field 20'

J. Corder

NGC 6397
10-inch
Field 25'

J. Corder

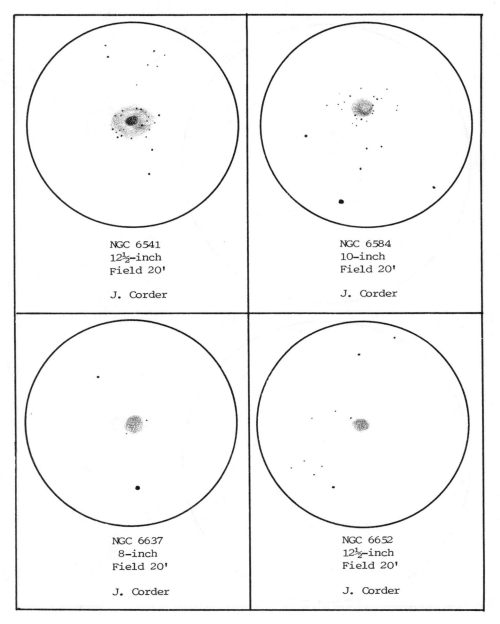

NGC 6541
12½-inch
Field 20'

J. Corder

NGC 6584
10-inch
Field 20'

J. Corder

NGC 6637
8-inch
Field 20'

J. Corder

NGC 6652
12½-inch
Field 20'

J. Corder

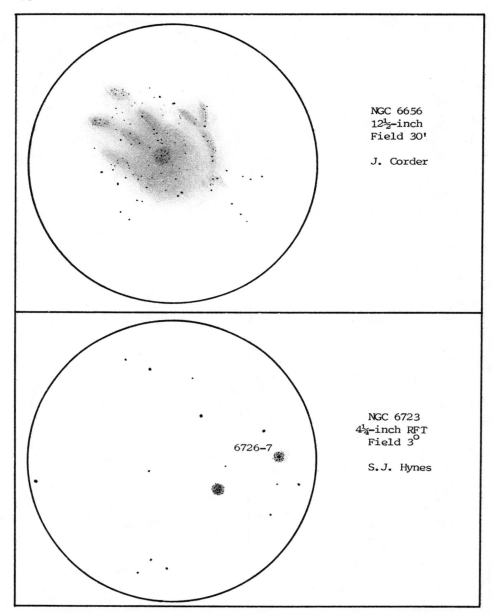

NGC 6656
12½-inch
Field 30'

J. Corder

NGC 6723
4¼-inch RFT
Field 3°

S.J. Hynes

6726-7

Catalogue

SECTION 3: PLANETARY NEBULAE

Data provided with this section:

(a) Catalogue number
(b) R.A. and Dec. for Epoch 2000.0
(c) Type (according to the classification system of Vorontsov-Velyaminov)
(d) Apparent magnitude of nebulosity
(e) Apparent magnitude of central star
(f) Size (in seconds of arc)
(g) Constellation

The data at (c) to (f) is taken from the Catalogue of Galactic Planetary Nebulae (Perek & Kohoutek, 1969), Atlas Coeli (Becvar, 1964) and Planetary Nebulae (Pottasch, 1984).

Note: A brief description of the Vorontsov-Velyaminov classification system is given in the 'Handbook', Volume 2, page 51.

Observers and Accredited Objects

NGC	246	– MJT	NGC 6026	– JC
	1360	– JC	6072	– JC, RJM
	1535	– MJT	6153	– RJM, JC, VH
IC	418	– MJT, JC, ESB	IC 4634	– JC
IC	2165	– JC, ESB	IC 4637	– JC
NGC	2438	– SJH, JC	M 2-9	– DAA
	2440	– JC, KGJ	NGC 6326	– JC
	2452	– JC, RJM	6337	– RJB, JC
M	3-4	– DAA	M 2-13	– DAA
M	3-5	– DAA	NGC 6369	– RJM, JC
NGC	2610	– SS	Hubble 4	– DAA
	2792	– JC, RJM	IC 4663	– JC
	2818	– MJT, JC	NGC 6445	– MJT, RJM, JC
	2867	– JC	6563	– JC, RJM
	2899	– VH	6565	– JC
	3132	– RJM, JC, VH	6567	– JC, PB
	3242	– MJT, KGJ, VH	6629	– JC, RJM
	3918	– JC	6644	– JC
	4361	– JC, PB	IC 4776	– JC
	5307	– JC	NGC 6818	– VH
IC	4406	– RJM	7009	– MJT, JC, KGJ
NGC	5882	– RJM, JC	7293	– MJT, JC, PB
Me	2-1	– DAA, JC, PB		

(N.B. M = Minkowski, Me = Merrill).

Catalogue	R.A.	Dec.	Type	m(n)	m(s)	Size	Const
NGC 246	00 47.1	−11 53	IIIa	8.0	10.5	240x210	Cet

(16½) Annular; S. and S.p. edges brightest. Brighter area in
N.f. section. Four stars involved, the brightest being in the
N.p. part of the nebulosity.

NGC 1360	03 33.4	−25 51	III		11.3	418	For

(12½) Very large and bright with a prominent central star.
Very thick elliptical shape with a much brighter section
within, radiating S.E. from the central star.

NGC 1535	04 14.5	−12 44	IV+VI	9.6	10.0	20x17	Eri

(16½) Blue, irregularly round nebula. At x351, star
surrounded by dark mottling, enclosed by bright ring in
slightly elongated shell.

IC 418	05 27.7	−12 45	IV	12.0	9.0	14x11	Lep

(16½) At x84 seen as a bright star in a small nebula.
Slightly elongated N.p./S.f. when observed at x351, and at
x527 a dark area and bright outer ring.
(12½) Slightly elliptical; elongated N – S. An annulus with
a bright central star, estimated to be mag. 11.
(8½) At x 204 seen as a very bright oval with no sign of
annularity. Stellar at low-power.

Catalogue	R.A.	Dec.	Type	m(n)	m(s)	Size	Const.
IC 2165	06 21.9	-12 59	IIIb	12.5	18.5	8	CMa

(12½) Very small and very bright (est. mag. 11); elongated
N - S. Bluish in colour and of a thick lenticular shape.
Non-stellar at x107.
(8½) Easy object at x204. Elliptical in P.A. $90^{\circ} - 270^{\circ}$.
Produces a bright prism image at x102.

NGC 2438	07 41.8	-14 43	IV	9.7	17.7	68	Pup

Involved in open cluster NGC 2437 (M.46).

(8½) A small colourless nebula, about 40" diameter, on N. edge
of NGC 2437. Seen without difficulty at x77; est. mag. 11.
Circular, with no evidence of annularity or a central star.
Nebula adjacent to star of similar magnitude.

NGC 2440	07 42.2	-18 13	V+III	9.1		54x20	Pup

(8) Very bright and small (about 25" x 20"), somewhat
flattened and elongated E - W. Edges fuzzy and diffuse.

NGC 2452	07 47.4	-27 21	IV+III	12.6	18.0	20	Pup

(12½) Small, bright elliptical PN of est. mag. 12. In same
field as a small, rich open cluster 10' N. (NGC 2453).
(8) Small, faint and round. Close to a small triangle of
slightly brighter stars and S. of the hazy, irregular cluster
NGC 2453.

M 3-4	07 55.2	-23 24	IV				Pup

(60) Faint. Diameter 20" - 25". No central star seen.

Catalogue	R.A.	Dec.	Type	m(n)	m(s)	Size	Const
M 3–5	08 02.6	–27 40	IV			7	Pup

(40) Oval nebula of even illumination. Star on N.E. edge.

Catalogue	R.A.	Dec.	Type	m(n)	m(s)	Size	Const
NGC 2610	08 33.6	–16 08	IV+II	13.6	15.5	35	Hya

(8) A difficult low-power object but at x145, the slightly brighter centre shows signs of mottling. Edges ill-defined at x362. Star on N.f. edge.

Catalogue	R.A.	Dec.	Type	m(n)	m(s)	Size	Const
NGC 2792	09 12.5	–42 26	IV	13.5	13.8	13	Vel

(12½) Bright and very easy (est. mag. 11.5). Very small and elliptical, aligned N.W. – S.E.
(10) Very small, round, slightly greenish disc. Even brightness throughout. No central star seen.
(8) Stellar.

Catalogue	R.A.	Dec.	Type	m(n)	m(s)	Size	Const
NGC 2818	09 16.0	–36 36	IIIb	13.0	17.5	50	Pyx

Involved in open cluster NGC 2818A.

(16½) PN contained within an open cluster, being slightly p. the centre of the cluster. At x84, the planetary is easily visible, showing an oval disc which becomes elongated S.p. – N.f. when examined at x176, the ends of major axis brightening. This is confirmed at x351, when the central area is dark and mottled.
(12½) Fine, bright, thick elliptical nebula at N. edge of coarse open cluster NGC 2818A. The planetary, which is of about mag. 12, measures approx. 90" x 60" in size.

Catalogue	R.A.	Dec.	Type	m(n)	m(s)	Size	Const
NGC 2867	09 21.4	−58 18	IIIb	9.7	14.4	15	Car

(12½) Very small and bright. Elliptical; elongated N.W. − S.E.

Catalogue	R.A.	Dec.	Type	m(n)	m(s)	Size	Const
NGC 2899	09 27.1	−56 08				120	Vel

(6) Hazy, luminous spot with a slightly brighter centre.

Catalogue	R.A.	Dec.	Type	m(n)	m(s)	Size	Const
NGC 3132	10 07.1	−40 25	IV	8.2	10.1	56	Vel

Central star binary.

(10) Very large elliptical envelope, slightly bluish in colour. Bright, condensed core, but not clearly stellar.
(6) Bright oval nebula, best seen at x115. Even brightness with a bright central star. About 50" in diameter.

Catalogue	R.A.	Dec.	Type	m(n)	m(s)	Size	Const
NGC 3242	10 24.8	−18 38	IIIb+IV	9.0	11.7	40x35	Hya

(16½) Very blue. Extended N.p. − S.f. At x527, two bright spots seen in inner shell. Edges of outer shell less well defined than inner.
(8) Bright blue oval, brighter to N.E. and N. Dark annulus around star, faint traces of outer ring. Mag. 10 star 5' S.f.
(6) Very bright nebula, slightly elongated N − S. Best seen at x114. No central star. About 50" diameter.

Catalogue	R.A.	Dec.	Type	m(n)	m(s)	Size	Const
NGC 3918	11 50.3	−57 10	IIb	8.4	13.4	15	Cen

(12½) Bright and easy. Very small and slightly oblate. Blue.

Catalogue	R.A.	Dec.	Type	m(n)	m(s)	Size	Const
NGC 4361	12 24.5	−18 46	IIIa	12.8	14.3	81	Crv

(8) Bright, pretty large and slightly elongated N.W. − S.E.
Even surface brightness.
(6) Faint, even nebulosity around star.

NGC 5307	13 51.1	−51 12	III	12.1		15x10	Cen

(10) Very small and very bright. Stellar at low powers but
at x300 seen to be slightly elliptical and about 5" across.
Even surface brightness.

IC 4406	14 22.5	−44 09	IIIb	10.6		100x37	Lup

(10) Small, bright disc of even brightness throughout.

NGC 5882	15 16.9	−45 38		10.5	13.1	14	Lup

(10) Small, bright, blue disc of even brightness throughout.
(6) Round, bright and very small, with a bluish tint
evident. Mag. 11 star about 8" N. Nebula brightens evenly to
centre.

Catalogue	R.A.	Dec.	Type	m(n)	m(s)	Size	Const
Me 2-1	15 22.3	-23 38	II	12.0	16.7	5	Lib

(100) Beautiful circular planetary, greeny-blue, 10" diameter. Uniform, sharp edges and no central star.
(12½) Round, bright and very small. Forms a pair with a star about 1' W. Non-stellar at x95.
(8) Definite grey disc seen at x205. Slight central brightening to a core of about mag. 12 - 13.

Catalogue	R.A.	Dec.	Type	m(n)	m(s)	Size	Const
NGC 6026	16 01.4	-34 33	IV	13.0		45	Lup

(10) Pretty faint oval nebula with a bright, prominent central star. Evenly bright.

Catalogue	R.A.	Dec.	Type	m(n)	m(s)	Size	Const
NGC 6072	16 13.0	-36 15	IIIa	14.1	19.1	70	Sco

(10) Bright and easy. Nearly round, fairly large and of even surface brightness. Lies between 2 stars W., and 4 stars E.
(8) Large, round and faint, but seen with direct vision. Slight brightening on W. edge. Edges sharp.

Catalogue	R.A.	Dec.	Type	m(n)	m(s)	Size	Const
NGC 6153	16 31.4	-40 14	I	11.5	16.1	24	Sco

(10) Very bright. Small, box-shaped or slightly oblate, and of even brightness but with fuzzy edges. Trio of bright stars immediately N. with which the PN forms a trapezium. Green colour sometimes apparent in 10-inch. PN just east of the open cluster NGC 6124.
(6) Just non-stellar at x73. Better seen at x114 and x230 when it appears very slightly elliptical. No central star.

Catalogue	R.A.	Dec.	Type	m(n)	m(s)	Size	Const
IC 4634	17 01.4	−21 49	IIa	12.0	17.0	20x10	Oph

(12½) Very small, bright and easy, est. mag. 10.0. Size about 6". Roundish, with 2 mag. 12 stars following.

IC 4637	17 05.1	−40 53	III	13.5		10	Sco

(10) Small and quite bright with fuzzy, ill-defined edges and an elongated shape. Forms a trapezium with 3 mag. 11 stars to N. and E. Decidedly non-stellar at x71.

M 2-9	17 05.8	−10 08	VI	10.0		15x9	Oph

(100) Mag. 13 star with jets of nebulosity, 15" to N. and 10" to S. More 'cometary' than 'planetary'.

NGC 6326	17 20.8	−51 45	IIIb	12.0	15.2	12	Ara

(10) Very small and egg-shaped (size about 5' x 6"). Very slightly brighter in the centre. Edges well defined with an extremely faint star noted at N.W. edge.

Catalogue	R.A.	Dec.	Type	m(n)	m(s)	Size	Const
NGC 6337	17 22.2	-38 28	IV	14.0	14.8	48	Sco

(40) Faint, slightly elliptical ring containing a faint central star. The rim of the nebula is weak on one side for about 60° and gradually brightens to a slightly higher surface brightness for the remainder of the circle. The interior of the ring is not dark. NGC 6337 lies in a rich starfield.
(10) Very faint, pretty small and not quite round. Evenly bright to the centre with two very faint stars on E. and W. edges.

Catalogue	R.A.	Dec.	Type	m(n)	m(s)	Size	Const
M 2-13	17 28.5	-13 25				10	Ser

(100) Blue star, suspected non-stellar.

Catalogue	R.A.	Dec.	Type	m(n)	m(s)	Size	Const
NGC 6369	17 29.3	-23 46	IV+II	11.0	16.0	28	Oph

(10) Disc with a darker centre and brighter, condensed area on N. side.
(8) Round and pretty bright with no central star. Evenly bright with sharply defined edges.

Catalogue	R.A.	Dec.	Type	m(n)	m(s)	Size	Const
Hubble 4	17 41.8	-21 42	IIIb	13.6		6	Oph

(100) Fluffy planetary, 8" in diameter, slightly elliptical in P.A. 50°. No central star.

Catalogue	R.A.	Dec.	Type	m(n)	m(s)	Size	Const
IC 4663	17 45.2	−44 54	IV	13.0	14.0	15	Sco

(12½) Pretty faint and very small (about 5"). Round, with a high surface brightness and sharply defined edges. String of 4 stars extends S.

Catalogue	R.A.	Dec.	Type	m(n)	m(s)	Size	Const
NGC 6445	17 49.3	−20 01	IIIb	9.5	19.1	38x29	Sgr

(16½) Annular; N. edge brightest. Nebula slightly extended N.p. − S.f.
(10) Elongated disc with a dark centre; disc appears to be bisected by a dark lane. Faint. Star close by.
(8) Round and of even surface brightness. Small and quite faint (est. mag. 10.5 − 11.0). Situated in a fairly rich field, 2 doubles close S.

Catalogue	R.A.	Dec.	Type	m(n)	m(s)	Size	Const
NGC 6563	18 12.0	−33 52	IIIa	14.0	17.0	45	Sgr

(10) Pretty bright and fairly small; of even brightness and somewhat rectangular in shape. Faint trio of stars S.S.E. Very bright field star 15' N.N.W.

Catalogue	R.A.	Dec.	Type	m(n)	m(s)	Size	Const
NGC 6565	18 11.9	−28 10	IV	13.0	19.2	10x8	Sgr

(10) Very bright and very small, about 3" x 4"; elongated E − W. Gradually brighter towards the centre. Lies in a rich field.

Catalogue	R.A.	Dec.	Type	m(n)	m(s)	Size	Const
NGC 6567	18 13.8	−19 04	IIa	11.7	15.5	11x7	Sgr

(10) Very small and bright. Round or very slightly oblate, with well defined edges. Even surface brightness. Mag. 12 star at S.E. edge. Situated in a rich Milky Way field.
(8) Slightly nebulous star at x125. At x310, slight elongation in P.A. 20° − 200°. Mag. 12 star almost in contact to E.

Catalogue	R.A.	Dec.	Type	m(n)	m(s)	Size	Const
NGC 6629	18 25.7	−23 12	IIa	10.5	12.7	15	Sgr

(10) Very small, bright, blue-green disc. Slightly brighter in the centre.
(8) Small and pretty bright elliptical nebula of even surface brightness. Elongated N − S. Mag. 12 star 20" S.

Catalogue	R.A.	Dec.	Type	m(n)	m(s)	Size	Const
NGC 6644	18 32.6	−25 09	II	12.2	11.5	2	Sgr

(10) Very small but decidedly non-stellar, about 4" x 5". Even surface brightness, with well defined edges. Two mag. 12 stars frame the nebula to the E. and W.

Catalogue	R.A.	Dec.	Type	m(n)	m(s)	Size	Const
IC 4776	18 45.8	−33 20	IIa	12.5	16.0	8x6	Sgr

(10) Extremely small, about 3" x 4", and pretty faint. Slightly elongated N.W. − S.E.

90

Catalogue	R.A.	Dec.	Type	m(n)	m(s)	Size	Const
NGC 6818	19 43.9	−14 10	IV	9.9	14.9	19	Sgr

(6) Clearly seen as a small, well defined, oval 'smoke ring'.
Best seen at x73.

Catalogue	R.A.	Dec.	Type	m(n)	m(s)	Size	Const
NGC 7009	21 04.2	−11 22	IV+IIIa	8.4	14.5	44x26	Aqr

(16½) Bright blue oval; inner bright disc in fainter nebula;
S. and S.p. sides brighter.
(12½) Extremely bright and quite large; very asymmetrical
shape, roughly elliptical and elongated E − W, with a faint
'spike' extending 10" W. A bright 'knob', 2" − 3" E. also
noted.
(8) Bright oval, P.A. 70° − 150°; solid outline and traces of
ansae. No star seen.

Catalogue	R.A.	Dec.	Type	m(n)	m(s)	Size	Const
NGC 7293	22 29.7	−20 51	IV	6.5	13.3	900x720	Aqr

(16½) Annular. Ring very wide and broken on N.p. edge.
Brighter on N.f. and S. edges. Two stars at centre.
(12½) Fairly bright and very large, being of an irregularly
elliptical shape, elongated N.W. − S.E. Centre diffuse.
Central star easily seen, as also a nearby star.
(4¼) Very large and easy, though not bright. Not quite
round, slightly elongated E − W. Centre noticeably darker.
Three stars on W. edge.

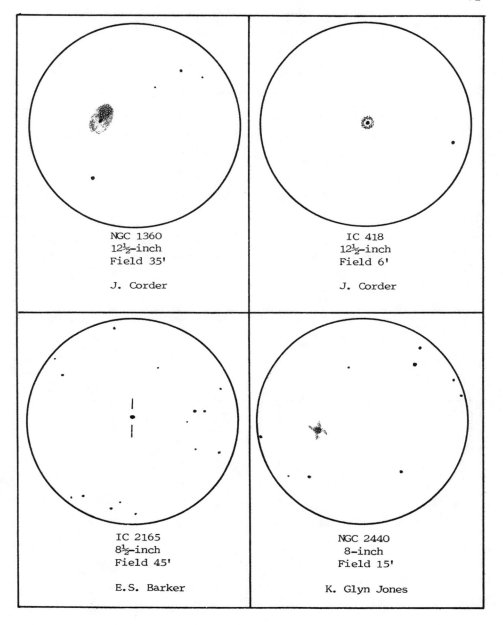

NGC 1360
12½-inch
Field 35'

J. Corder

IC 418
12½-inch
Field 6'

J. Corder

IC 2165
8½-inch
Field 45'

E.S. Barker

NGC 2440
8-inch
Field 15'

K. Glyn Jones

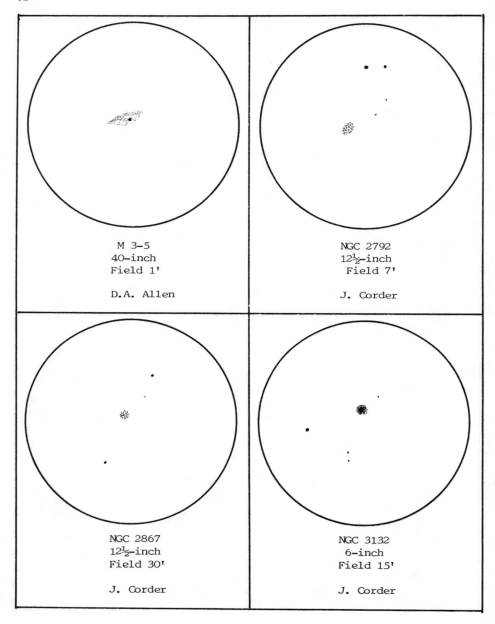

M 3-5
40-inch
Field 1'

D.A. Allen

NGC 2792
12½-inch
Field 7'

J. Corder

NGC 2867
12½-inch
Field 30'

J. Corder

NGC 3132
6-inch
Field 15'

J. Corder

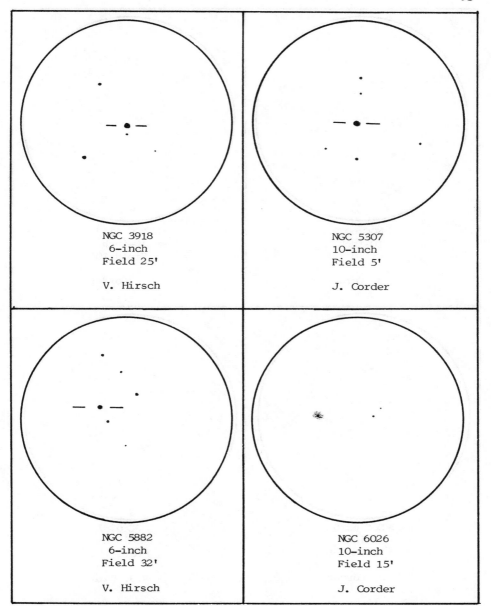

NGC 3918
6-inch
Field 25'

V. Hirsch

NGC 5307
10-inch
Field 5'

J. Corder

NGC 5882
6-inch
Field 32'

V. Hirsch

NGC 6026
10-inch
Field 15'

J. Corder

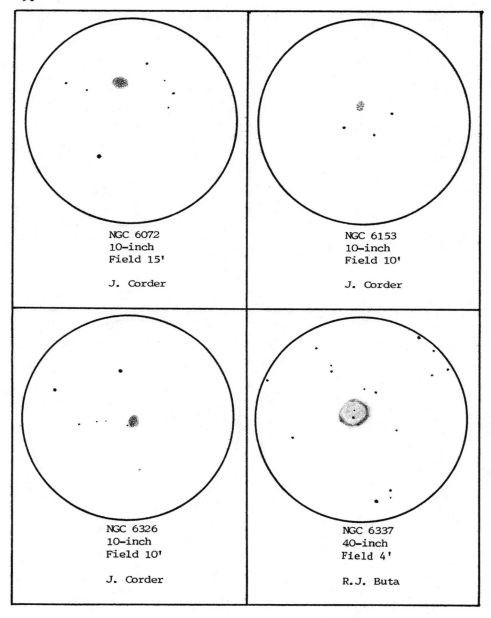

NGC 6072
10-inch
Field 15'

J. Corder

NGC 6153
10-inch
Field 10'

J. Corder

NGC 6326
10-inch
Field 10'

J. Corder

NGC 6337
40-inch
Field 4'

R.J. Buta

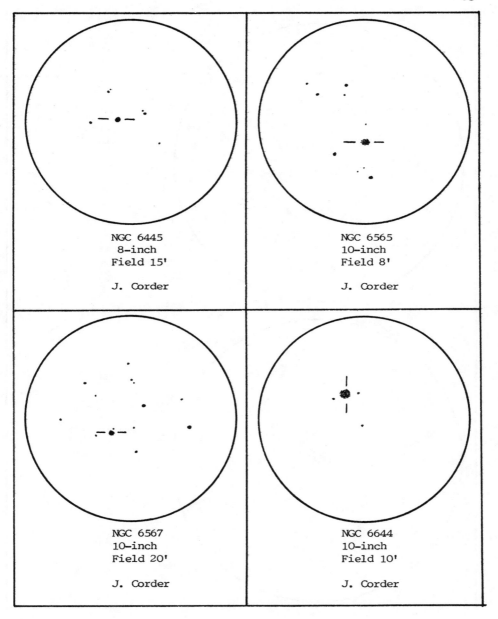

NGC 6445
8-inch
Field 15'

J. Corder

NGC 6565
10-inch
Field 8'

J. Corder

NGC 6567
10-inch
Field 20'

J. Corder

NGC 6644
10-inch
Field 10'

J. Corder

96

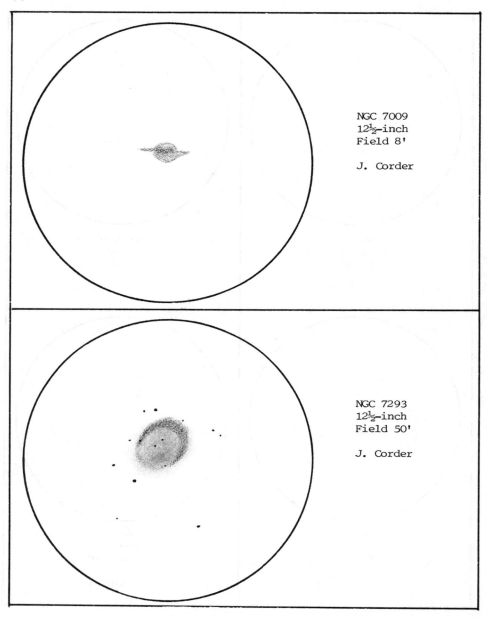

NGC 7009
12½-inch
Field 8'

J. Corder

NGC 7293
12½-inch
Field 50'

J. Corder

Catalogue

SECTION 4: DIFFUSE NEBULAE

Data provided with this section:

(a) Catalogue number
(b) R.A. and Dec. for Epoch 2000.0
(c) Type (E = emission, R = reflection)
(d) Size (in minutes of arc)
(e) Apparent magnitude of exciting star
(f) Constellation

The data in (c) to (e) is taken from Atlas Coeli (Becvar, 1964)

Observers and Accredited Objects

NGC 2327	– MJT	NGC 4605	– VH
2359	– MJT	6302	– DAA, RJB, JC
2467	– MJT, JC, VH	6334	– JC
2626	– JC	6357	– JC
3199	– JC	6514	– DAA, JC, SJH
3324	– JC, VH	B.86	– JC, RJM
3372	– CH, JC, VH	NGC 6523	– MJT, SJH
3581–2	– JC, VH	NGC 6559)	– MJT, JC, VH
IC 2944	– VH	IC 4681)	
NGC 5367	– JC	NGC 6589–90 – MJT	
IC 4592	– ESB, VH	6618	– SJH, VH
		6726–7–9	– JC, SJH

Catalogue	R.A.	Dec.	Type	Size	m(s)	Const
NGC 2327	07 04.3	−11 18	R	20	10.0	CMa

(16½) Irregular, small nebula surrounding a double star, the brightest portion p. the northern of the two stars.

Catalogue	R.A.	Dec.	Type	Size	m(s)	Const
NGC 2359	07 17.7	−13 12	E	8x6	11.0	CMa

IC 468 is the fainter N.W. portion of this nebula.

(16½) Entire nebula visible, NGC 2359 appearing as a bright wedge along the southern edge. Many stars involved.

Catalogue	R.A.	Dec.	Type	Size	m(s)	Const
NGC 2467	07 53.4	−26 24	E	4	8.5	Pup

(16½) Very large, bright and irregularly round nebula in a rich starfield. Quite a few stars involved with the nebulosity itself, including a bright one just inside the northern edge. Resembles a large, ring-type planetary nebula with the ring being wide and appearing brighter on the S.p. edge. When examined at x176 it is a beautiful sight, the central area being large and quite dark while the S. and S.p. areas consist of brighter nebulosity.
(12½) Pretty bright nebula (about mag. 11), nearly round in shape but slightly elongated N.W. − S.E. Northern end brighter with mag. 8 star immersed. Gradually fades towards south and west with W. side being most indistinct.
(6) Slightly oval, ill-defined nebula, centred on a mag. 8 star. Rather faint to direct vision but better seen using a nebular filter. Size estimated at 6' x 5'.

Catalogue	R.A.	Dec.	Type	Size	m(s)	Const
NGC 2626	08 35.6	−40 38	R		9.4	Vel

(12½) Fairly small (4' x 3'.5) diffuse nebula with a mag. 10 star near N. side. Roughly fan-shaped or thickly oblate, fading towards the south very gradually. Fairly bright and easy (about mag. 12).

Catalogue	R.A.	Dec.	Type	Size	m(s)	Const
NGC 3199	10 16.9	−57 57	R			Car

(12½) Very large. Roughly U-shaped; brightest section toward
S.W., orientated N − S, with a bright star at N. end and
measures 7' x 4'. Fainter section, N.E., orientated E − W,
measures 20' x 5' and contains 8 stars with a bright star at
E. end. Nebula generally evenly faint.

NGC 3324	10 37.4	−58 38	E	15x14	8.4	Car

(12½) Double nebula, pretty large and faint. Diffuse, with
even surface brightness. Nebula to S. contains 2 pretty
bright stars.
(6) Very faint, ill-defined nebula with a mag. 8 star
associated. Better seen with nebular filter.

NGC 3372 η Car.	10 45.0	−59 41	E	85x80	var	Car

(12) Using x200, the shape of the 'Homunculus' nebula, around
the η Car. star itself, is easily discerned. A narrow dark
lane can be seen on the torso of the 'Homunculus'.
(6) A beautiful and extremely large nebulous complex! Fine
mixture of stars, bright nebulae and dark lanes. Contains a
rich association of stars extending mostly N − S with bright
elongated nebulosity, brightest to the west. Five main areas
of nebulosity noted with the brightest and smallest
containing η Car.
(4½) A beautiful nebula, looking like a thumb-smear of light,
with many stars shining through. One particularly orange
star dominates. The dark lanes in the nebula well seen.
(12x40) Nebula of complicated structure, penetrated by dark
lanes of obscuring matter and divided into regions of
different brightness. The area is very rich in faint stars.

Catalogue	R.A.	Dec.	Type	Size	m(s)	Const
NGC 3581-2	11 12.1	-61 18	R		9.2	Car

Several other neb. patches in area, incl. NGC 3579-84-86.

(12½) NGC 3581 is a faint, pretty large fan-shaped nebula with
a mag. 9 star at S. apex. Orientated N.N.E. - S.S.W. Forms
a pair with NGC 3582, which is a small, very faint nebula of
a thick wedge-shape, 8' E. of 3581. NGC 3582 contains two
stars (mag. 9 & 11) and is orientated E - W, size 3' x 5'.
(6) Small fan shaped nebula with a mag. 9 star at the apex,
which points S. Faint. In the same x32 field, S.p. 3581, is
a smaller, considerably fainter nebulosity.

IC 2944	11 35.8	-63 01	R	66x36	3.3	Cen

----

(6) Oval nebula of about 10' to 15' extent, surrounding λ Cen.
Fades evenly into the background.

NGC 5367	13 57.7	-39 58				Cen

----

(6) A system of faint and small nebulae around 3 bright
mag. 7/8 stars. Nebulae about 3' in diameter and round.

IC 4592	16 12.1	-19 28	R	175x45	4.2	Sco

(8½) Faint nebula around ν Sco. and its companion,
 extending furthest to S.W. and N.E.; possibly a dark lane to
S.E.
(6) Nebula around the wide double ν Sco.; clearly seen at x73
and x114. Elongated roughly N - S.

Catalogue	R.A.	Dec.	Type	Size	m(s)	Const
IC 4605	16 30.0	–25 09	R	60x40	4.9	Sco

(6) Small nebula around 22 Sco. A fainter star N.W. may also be involved.

Catalogue	R.A.	Dec.	Type	Size	m(s)	Const
NGC 6302	17 13.8	–37 07	E	4x1.5	10.0	Sco

(40) The central part is a bright elliptical blob perhaps 20'' across. Around this is a fainter region which gives the impression of violent activity. Jets and streamers seem to radiate from the central area. There is no visible star associated with the nebula, which is greenish in colour and about 6' x 2'.

(36) An elongated, high surface brightness nebula with three distinct sections connected by fainter nebulosity. Two narrow arcs are visible emerging toward each other from the ends of the bright elliptical section on one end, and nearly form a ring. From each of the other two sections a straight narrow streak of nebulosity emerges and extends for quite some distance. These are nearly parallel and neither is especially conspicuous.

($12\frac{1}{2}$) Bright and pretty small nebula with a bright elongated core area and an irregular jet extending S.W. Outer nebulosity very faint and tenuous.

Catalogue	R.A.	Dec.	Type	Size	m(s)	Const
NGC 6334	17 20.6	–36 04	R	20x20	8.0	Sco

(10) Very faint nebula about 4' in diameter with a mag. 8 star at S.W. edge and an extremely faint star at N.E. edge. The nebula is evenly bright with very diffuse edges. Slightly oblate, being elongated N.E. – S.W.

Catalogue	R.A.	Dec.	Type	Size	m(s)	Const
NGC 6357	17 24.6	−34 10	E	57x44	10.0	Sco

(10) Small (3' x 2') but not difficult. Roughly pear-shaped with a mag. 10 double at narrow end; slightly brighter centre and rather indefinite edges. Aligned N.W. − S.E.

NGC 6514 M.20	18 02.4	−23 02	E+R	30x25	6.9	Sgr

Trifid Nebula.

(100, 60) Surprisingly faint for a Messier object; it is large and milky, and does not seem to brighten very much towards the centre; three prominent dark lanes, almost evenly spaced 120° apart, radiate from the central multiple star. (8) Fine bright double star at convergence of dark lanes. The nebula is of even brightness and is best observed with low power; mostly faint with a three-lobed structure. (4¼ RFT) Not very prominent. Appears as a small circular nebula with a star at the centre. The larger, much brighter M.8 can just be included in the same 3° field.

B.86	18 03.5	−27 54		4.5x3.0		Sgr

Dark nebula. OCl. NGC 6520 adjacent.

(10) Inky spot in the Milky Way. Irregularly elongated and somewhat box-shaped, with a bright golden star at N. end. Two very faint stars noted inside the nebula, on E. side. (8) Irregularly oblong dark nebula elongated N − S, clearly seen to W. of NGC 6520. Three obvious stars seen within the nebula. A bright chain of stars seen just outside, and to W. of nebula, elongated N − S.

Catalogue	R.A.	Dec.	Type	Size	m(s)	Const
NGC 6523	18 03.7	−24 23	E	55x35	6.8	Sgr
M.8	Lagoon Nebula.					

(16½) Over 30' across. The dark lane curves across from
N.W. – S.E. and is quite wide. The W. section of the nebula
is mottled and the 'Hourglass' seen as a bright arc.
(4¼ RFT) Even at x16 seen to be a very complex nebula system.
Within an oval, faintly luminous glow over a degree in
diameter are three main areas of brightness. The main
component is roughly circular and is p. the southernmost of
2 fairly bright stars. The space between this and the
second brightest component is the lane which gives the nebula
its popular name; the fainter components are rather elongated.
The cluster NGC 6530 is involved: this includes at least a
dozen stars, several in pairs.

NGC 6559	18 09.9	−24 07	E	8x5	9.8	Sgr
& IC 4681						

(16½) Large and fairly bright. A curved arc, broader and
brighter at N.p. end, where two stars are involved, the
brightest being a double.
(10) Easy but faint nebula with 2 mag. 10 stars immersed
N – S at centre. Extensions to N. and S.
(6) A faint, oval nebula surrounded on N.E. side by a
clustering of faint stars, trailing like a necklace with a
brighter 'pendant' star at the southern end.

NGC 6589	18 16.9	−19 40	R	5x3	9.5	Sgr
NGC 6590			R	3x2	10.0	

(16½) NGC 6589 appears merely as a faint, irregular nebula
enveloping 2 stars. NGC 6590 is a bright oval nebula
containing 2 stars of equal magnitude.

Catalogue	R.A.	Dec.	Type	Size	m(s)	Const
NGC 6618 M.17	18 20.9 Omega Nebula.	−16 11	E	50x40		Sgr

($8\frac{1}{2}$) A long, bright bar of nebulosity slightly S.p. a small
clustering of stars. Variable in brightness but most
prominent about 5' S.f. a fairly bright star, which the
nebula appeared to envelope. At N. end of nebula, around the
star, the nebula comes to a blunt end, with a small tongue of
nebulosity curling around the star.
($4\frac{1}{4}$) Bright and easy nebula plus a nearby cluster of 9 fairly
bright stars. Elongated patch roughly E – W, 15' long and 5'
wide. Brightness falls off sharply at N. edge of nebula.

NGC 6726– 7–9	19 01.8 involves variables R and TY CrA.	−36 54	E+R		var.	CrA

----

(10) Fine, easy region of nebulae and 3 bright stars.
NGC 6726–7 connected and both appear roundish with mag. 8 & 9
stars at the centres; nebulae of basically even surface
brightness. NGC 6729 noted about 10' to S., with mag. 11
central star and appearing fainter than the NGC 6726–7 pair.
($4\frac{1}{4}$ RFT) In the same 3° field as the globular cluster NGC 6723
is a string of bright stars including CrA. One of the
brightest of these is surrounded by a bright nebulous halo,
the most prominent section of the nebula (NGC 6726).

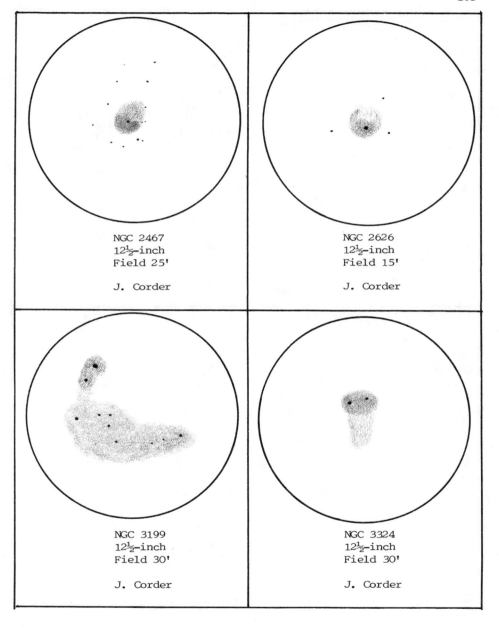

NGC 2467
12½-inch
Field 25'

J. Corder

NGC 2626
12½-inch
Field 15'

J. Corder

NGC 3199
12½-inch
Field 30'

J. Corder

NGC 3324
12½-inch
Field 30'

J. Corder

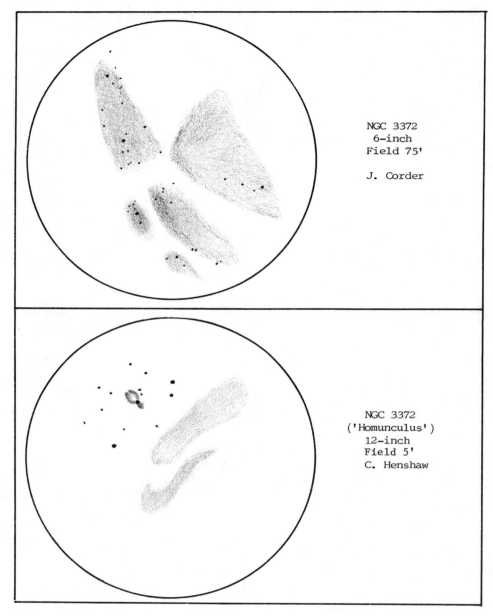

NGC 3372
6-inch
Field 75'

J. Corder

NGC 3372
('Homunculus')
12-inch
Field 5'
C. Henshaw

107

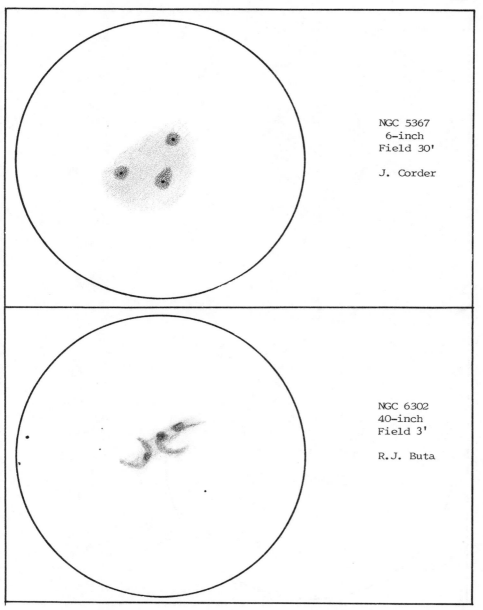

NGC 5367
6-inch
Field 30'

J. Corder

NGC 6302
40-inch
Field 3'

R.J. Buta

108

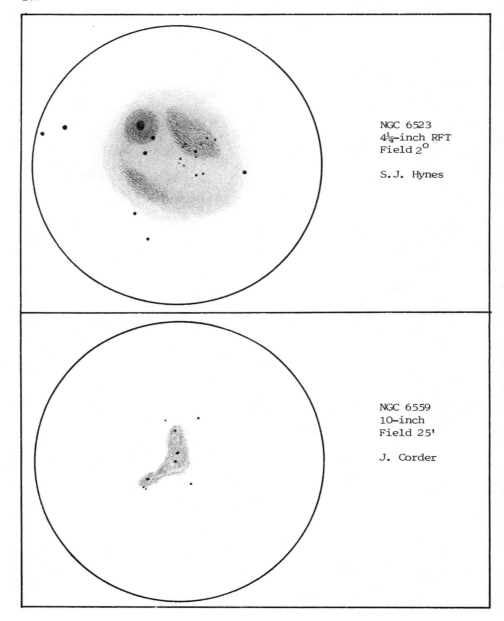

NGC 6523
4¼-inch RFT
Field 2°

S.J. Hynes

NGC 6559
10-inch
Field 25'

J. Corder

Catalogue

SECTION 5: GALAXIES

Data provided with this section:

(a) Catalogue number
(b) R.A. and Dec. for Epoch 2000.0
(c) Apparent magnitude
(d) Size (in minutes of arc)
(e) Type
(f) Constellation

The data in (c) and (d) is taken from Burnham's Celestial Handbook (Burnham, 1978) and the Revised New General Catalogue (Sulentic & Tifft, 1973). The data in (e) is taken from the Revised Shapley-Ames Catalogue of Galaxies (Sandage & Tammann, 1981). In a number of cases, additional information will be found on the line below the basic data.

Note: modern galaxy classification systems are described in the 'Handbook', Volume 4, page 10 - 14.

Observers and Accredited Objects

NGC	24	– JC, DBB	NGC	1365	– RJB, VH, DBB
	55	– RJM, VH		1374	– DBB
	134	– DBB		1379	– RJM, DBB
	148	– DBB		1380	– RJM, DBB
	150	– DBB		1381	– DBB
	175	– DBB		1386	– RJM, DBB
	247	– JC, DBB		1395	– JC
	253	– MJT, RJM, SJH		1398	– JC
	254	– DBB		1399	– JC, DBB
	289	– DBB		1404	– JC, DBB
	300	– JC, DBB		1406	– JC
	908	– JC		1411	– JC
	1097	– DAA, JC		1415	– JC
	1249	– JC		1425	– JC
	1291	– VH		1427	– DBB
	1313	– RJB		1433	– RJB
	1316	– VH, DBB		1437	– DBB
	1317	– VH, DBB		1448	– RJB
	1325	– VH		1512	– RJB
	1326	– DBB		1515	– JC
	1341	– DBB		1549	– JC
	1350	– VH, DBB		1553	– JC

Catalogue

NGC 1566	– RJB	NGC 5236	– RJM, VH, CH
1792	– VH	5253	– RJM
1964	– JC	IC 4329(G)	– JC
2188	– JC	NGC 5530	– JC
2217	– JC	AP Librae	– DAA
2283	– MJT	NGC 6215	– RJB
2292	– MJT	6221	– RJB
2295	– MJT	6300	– RJB
2427	– JC	6438	– RJB
2784	– JC	6744	– RJB
2997	– JC	6769-70-71	– RJB
3001	– JC	6822	– JC, ESB
3109	– RJM	7172(G)	– JC
3271(G)	– JC	7204	– RJB
3347(G)	– JC	7314	. JC
3621	– VH	7412	– JC
3783	– JC	7424	– RJB
4594	– SJH	7496	– RJB
4650	– DAA	7531	– RJB
4945	– JC, VH	7702	– RJB
5102	– JC	7713	– RJB
5128	– DAA, MJT, DD, VH	7793	– JC

Note: objects with the annotation (G) are galaxies within a group of galaxies, other members of which are described under the same heading.

Catalogue	R.A.	Dec.	mag.	Size	Type	Const.
NGC 24	00 10.0	−24 59	12.0	4.5x0.9	Sc(s)II-III	Scl

(12½) Very bright. Lenticular in shape with a bright elongated nucleus. Very thin, almost a streak. Mag. 13 star at E. tip. (6) Faint but distinct. Appears slightly elliptical and brighter toward the centre. Best seen with a.v.

| NGC 55 | 00 15.0 | −39 13 | 8.0 | 25x4 | Sc | Scl |

Member of Sculptor group.

(8) Very large and bright. Has a bright core and a very much extended outer envelope. Similar to NGC 253 and almost as impressive.
(6) A large, elongated nebula. It has a slight bulge in the centre and is brighter at the northern end. Inclined in P.A. 110°.

| NGC 134 | 00 30.3 | −33 16 | 11.0 | 5x1 | Sbc(s)II-III | Scl |

(6) At x70, seen as a faint but distinct elliptical nebula. Best seen with a.v.

| NGC 148 | 00 34.3 | −31 48 | 13.0 | 1.2x0.5 | S02(r)(6) | Scl |

(6) Fairly small but very distinct. Rather condensed.

| NGC 150 | 00 34.3 | −27 49 | 12.5 | 2x1 | Sbc(s)II | Scl |

(6) Very faint elliptical object, well seen with a.v.

112

Catalogue	R.A.	Dec.	mag.	Size	Type	Const.
NGC 175	00 37.4	−19 56	13.0	1.5x1.3	SBab(r)I-II	Cet

(6) Fairly distinct oval object, well seen with a.v.

Catalogue	R.A.	Dec.	mag.	Size	Type	Const.
NGC 247	00 47.1	−20 45	10.0	18x5	Sc(s)III-IV	Cet

Member of Sculptor group.

(12½) Extremely large. A thick lens with rounded ends,
measuring some 16' x 4'. Very little central brightening
noted. Mag. 12 star just off S. tip and an e.f. star immersed
S. of centre, on W. side.
(6) Fairly bright nebulous streak running approx. N-S, with a
distinct central bulge. The object has a noticeable 'spur' on
N. edge and at the other end a.v. reveals an arc feature.

Catalogue	R.A.	Dec.	mag.	Size	Type	Const.
NGC 253	00 47.5	−25 50	7.5	22x6	Sc(s)	Scl

Member of Sculptor group. SN 1940E.

(16½) Extremely large and greatly elongated S.p.-N.f. The
central area is non-stellar, being extended in the direction
of the major axis. Considerable mottling is evident, dark
absorption patches being easily visible throughout the galaxy,
especially along the N. edge of the p. extension.
(8) A very extended envelope with a fairly well defined edge,
except for the extremities which gradually fade away. The
mid-section of the galaxy is large and very bright and
contains a small, round, brighter area which is more like a
bright knot than a core. Three stars involved.
(4¼ RFT) Easily found at x16 as a bright streak of nebulosity
about 20' x 5'. No distinct nucleus seen; however, the object
seems brighter at a point immediately following a bright star
close to it.

Catalogue	R.A.	Dec.	mag.	Size	Type	Const.
NGC 254	00 47.6	−31 26	13.0	1.3x0.5	RSO1(6)/Sa	Scl

----

(6) A fairly bright oval object adjacent to a bright field star.

| NGC 289 | 00 52.8 | −31 13 | 12.0 | 2x1.5 | SBbc(rs)I-II | Scl |

----

(6) Bright elliptical object, no details visible.

| NGC 300 | 00 55.0 | −37 42 | 10.0 | 21x14 | ScII.8 | Scl |

Member of Sculptor group.

(12½) Faint, extremely large and much elongated with a large bulging elliptical nucleus and core region. Star of mag. 11 at centre – possibly a stellar nucleus. Ends appear rounded with only slight tapering. Overall size about 20' x 5' and core about 6' x 5'.
(6) Rather elusive with only the central region being seen, this appearing as a soft elliptical object.
(15x80) A very large, low surface brightness object, becoming brighter in the centre and with a small slightly stellar nucleus. Has an apparent bar feature.

| NGC 908 | 02 23.1 | −21 13 | 10.9 | 4x1.3 | Sc(s)I-II | Cet |

(12½) A bright and fairly large elliptical object, evenly bright except for a much elongated, very bright nucleus, which appears somewhat displaced, N. of centre. Very faint star noted at S.W. edge.

114

Catalogue	R.A.	Dec.	mag.	Size	Type	Const.
NGC 1097	02 46.4	−30 16	10.5	9x5.5	RSBbc(rs)I-II	For

RNGC lists mag. 14 anon. companion. Arp 77. PKS 0244-304.

(154) Bright oval with spiral arms. Many individual clusters
and H II regions clearly seen in the arms, which could be
traced out for many minutes of arc. A small companion galaxy
lies within these arms.
(12½) Large, very much elongated and appears slightly
lenticular. Has a very much brighter oblate core and nucleus.

Catalogue	R.A.	Dec.	mag.	Size	Type	Const.
NGC 1249	03 10.0	−53 20	12.0	4x2	SBc(s)II	Hor

(12½) Very large and faint and of low surface brightness.
Elliptical in shape. No nucleus observed. Three easy stars
encompass the galaxy.

Catalogue	R.A.	Dec.	mag.	Size	Type	Const.
NGC 1291	03 17.3	−41 06	9.4	5x2	SBa	Eri

(6) Rather like a small globular, NGC 1291 is a small, round,
bright object with a brighter stellar nucleus. To N. of galaxy
is a star of similar magnitude to the nucleus.

Catalogue	R.A.	Dec.	mag.	Size	Type	Const.
NGC 1313	03 18.3	−66 29	10.5	5x3.2	SBc(s)III-IV	Ret

RNGC lists anon. companion. SN 1962M.

(40) A very diffuse, broad bar of relatively low surface
brightness. Emerging from one end of this is a faint arc
which ends in an elongated patch. Near the opposite end of
the bar is a large, round diffuse knot, and some distance
further is a second. Both knots appear detached from the main
body of the galaxy.

Catalogue	R.A.	Dec.	mag.	Size	Type	Const.
NGC 1316	03 22.5	−37 15	10.5	3.5x2.5	Sa pec.	For

RNGC lists 3 anon. companions. Fornax A. Arp 154. SN 1980L, 1981E. Dominant member of Fornax cluster of galaxies.

----

(6) Elliptical nebula of high surface brightness. NGC 1317 in same field, about 8' N.
(5) Very bright and large elliptical object, with a bright almost star-like centre.

NGC 1317	03 22.6	−37 07	12.5	0.7x0.6	Sa	For

Fornax cluster.

----

(6) Smaller and fainter than nearby NGC 1316 and rather more ill-defined.
(5) In same field of view as NGC 1316 but smaller and fainter. Oval in shape.

NGC 1325	03 24.5	−21 32	12.3	3x1	Sb	Eri

RNGC lists mag. 13.5 anon. companion. SN 1975S.

----

(6) Faint, elongated object of indeterminate size, best seen with a.v.

NGC 1326	03 23.8	−36 29	11.5	3x2.5	RSBa	For

RNGC lists 2 anon. companions. Fornax cluster.

----

(5) Fairly bright and distinct. Clearly elliptical in shape and uniformly bright.

Catalogue	R.A.	Dec.	mag.	Size	Type	Const.
NGC 1341	03 27.9	-37 09	13.1	0.8x0.7	SBc(s)II-III	For

Fornax cluster.

(5) Distinctly elongated, condensed and apparently brighter than mag. 13.1.

NGC 1350	03 31.1	-33 37	12.0	3x1.5	Sa(r)	For

Fornax cluster. SN 1959A.

(6) Small elliptical patch with a slightly brighter nucleus.
(5) A bright elongated object of uniform brightness, in an attractive field.

NGC 1365	03 33.6	-36 08	10.5	8x3.5	SBb(s)I	For

Fornax cluster. SN 1957C, 1983.

(30) Very bright and very large. A striking object, this galaxy shows the perfect structure of a two-armed barred spiral. The spiral structure is very distinct: 2 arms emerge perpendicularly from a diffuse, broad bar, with faint patches present at the ends of the bar. A large, round, mottled central bulge is present which has 2 ill-defined dark lanes cutting into it.
(6) At x32 appears as a large, faint nebulous patch with a bright nucleus. Outer nebulosity virtually disappears at x114, through lack of contrast, leaving just the elongated nucleus visible.
(5) Fairly bright and distinct. A 'bar' feature detected when using a.v.

NGC 1374	03 35.4	-35 14	12.5	0.8x0.8	E0	For

Fornax cluster.

(5) A distinct, slightly elliptical patch. Featureless.

Catalogue	R.A.	Dec.	mag.	Size	Type	Const
NGC 1379	03 36.1	−35 27	12.5	0.6x0.6	E0	For

Fornax cluster.

----

(8) Round and of even brightness. Slightly brighter than nearby NGC 1381 but fainter than NGC 1387.
(5) A distinct oval, the second of 5 galaxies in a 1° field.

Catalogue	R.A.	Dec.	mag.	Size	Type	Const
NGC 1380	03 36.6	−34 59	11.5	3x1	SO3(7)/Sa	For

Fornax cluster. RNGC lists edge-on anon. companion.

----

(8) Elliptical with a brighter, fuzzy core. Core more conspicuous than most of the other nearby galaxies.
(5) Bright lenticular system with a bright stellar centre.

Catalogue	R.A.	Dec.	mag.	Size	Type	Const
NGC 1381	03 36.6	−35 18	13.0	2x0.5	SO1(10)	For

Fornax cluster.

----

(5) Distinctly elliptical but rather faint. Forms an obvious trio with NGC 1380 and nearby NGC 1382.

Catalogue	R.A.	Dec.	mag.	Size	Type	Const
NGC 1386	03 36.9	−36 00	12.5	2.5x1.0	Sa	Eri

Fornax cluster.

----

(8) Small and faint. Extended (cigar-shaped), with a possible brighter core.
(5) Small, slightly elliptical object.

118

Catalogue	R.A.	Dec.	mag.	Size	Type	Const.
NGC 1395	03 38.5	–23 02	11.5	1.5x1.0	E2	Eri

(12½) Pretty faint with a very bright nucleus. Small and elliptical.

NGC 1398	03 38.9	–26 20	11.0	4.5x3.8	SBab(r)I	For

(12½) Very bright and round with a much brighter middle.

NGC 1399	03 38.6	–35 27	10.9	1.4x1.4	E1	For

Fornax cluster.

(12½) Bright, nearly round, with a brighter nucleus. Forms a pair with NGC 1404.
(5) A very bright system, oval, becoming brighter to the centre. Forms a double system with NGC 1404.

NGC 1404	03 38.9	–35 35	11.5	1x1	E2	For

Fornax cluster.

(12½) Round, bright, with a brighter nucleus. Forms a pair with NGC 1399. Faint star 1' S.
(5) A distinct stellar centre surrounded by a soft nebulosity. A foreground star is found on S. edge of galaxy.

NGC 1406	03 39.5	–31 18	12.7	3x0.8	Sc(II)	For

(12½) Long, narrow streak with a slightly brighter elongated core. Pretty bright star N., 15" from W. tip.

Catalogue	R.A.	Dec.	mag.	Size	Type	Const.
NGC 1411	03 38.8	−44 05	12.0	1.4x1.1	SO2(4)	Hor

SN 1976L.

(6) A very small, very faint object, thickly elliptical in shape. Very slightly brighter towards the centre.

NGC 1415	03 40.9	−22 33	12.5	1.8x0.9	Sa/SBa	Eri

(12½) Small, bright and slightly elliptical with a brighter middle.

NGC 1425	03 42.1	−29 54	12.0	3.5x1.7	Sb(r)II	For

(12½) Elongated, with a bright nucleus. Easy, but smaller than expected.

NGC 1427	03 42.1	−35 24	12.5	1.4x1.0	E5	For

Fornax cluster. RNGC lists anon. companion.

(5) An indistinctly seen elliptical object.

NGC 1433	03 42.0	−47 14	11.0	7x6	SBb(s)I-II	Hor

(40) A bar surrounded by a general glow. At x200, traces of a ring enveloping the bar can be seen, but no more than a weak enhancement of the edge of the glow. Three bright spots visible within the nuclear ring.
(16) Bar clearly visible while nuclear region appears bright and non-stellar.

Catalogue	R.A.	Dec.	mag.	Size	Type	Const.
NGC 1437	03 43.6	−35 51	12.9	2x1.5	Sc(s)II	Eri

Fornax cluster.

----

(6) Small but very distinctive object with a slightly stellar
centre. Oval in shape.

| NGC 1448 | 03 44.6 | −44 38 | 11.5 | 6x1.1 | Sc(II) | Hor |

SN 1983.

----

(40) An enormous edge−on spiral, overflowing the field at
x520. No distinct structural details visible although the
bulge appears elongated and is perhaps slightly mottled.

| NGC 1512 | 04 03.9 | −43 21 | 11.5 | 3x2.5 | SBb(rs)Ipec | Hor |

----

(36) At x500 the beautiful image of a 'theta' galaxy is
visible, that is, a bright bar enveloped by a faint, closed
elliptical ring. The ring is large and fills a good fraction
of the field of view. NGC 1510 seen nearby; this is a very
bright, round object, of fairly high surface brightness.

| NGC 1515 | 04 03.9 | −54 06 | 12.1 | 5x1.1 | Sb(s)II | Dor |

RNGC lists anon. companion.

(12½) Long, very thin ellipse, almost lens−like. Bright
elliptical nucleus, surrounded by a large core. A string of
5 faint stars lies N.f.

Catalogue	R.A.	Dec.	mag.	Size	Type	Const.
NGC 1549	04 15.8	-55 34	11.0	2.8x2.5	E2	Dor

(12½) A thick ellipse with a stellar nucleus and gradually brighter centre. Forms a pair with NGC 1553.

Catalogue	R.A.	Dec.	mag.	Size	Type	Const.
NGC 1553	04 16.3	-55 46	10.5	3.1x2.3	SO1/2(5)pec	Dor

(12½) Separated by about 10' from NGC 1549, NGC 1553 has an elliptical shape but is much thinner than its neighbour, with a larger, elongated nucleus. A bright star lies between the pair.

Catalogue	R.A.	Dec.	mag.	Size	Type	Const.
NGC 1566	04 20.0	-54 57	10.5	5x4	Sc(s)I	Dor

Seyfert galaxy. PKS 0418-550.

(40) One of the finest southern spirals. A small nucleus in a round, diffuse glow from which 2 extensive spiral arms emerge. One arm is particularly conspicuous and can be traced for nearly 180°. Near its furthest extent are two large elongated knots.

Catalogue	R.A.	Dec.	mag.	Size	Type	Const.
NGC 1792	05 05.1	-38 00	11.5	3x1	Sc(s)II	Col

(6) Nearly circular nebulosity with a slightly elongated brighter nucleus.

Catalogue	R.A.	Dec.	mag.	Size	Type	Const.
NGC 1964	05 33.3	-21 57	11.8	5x1.6	SbI-II	Lep

(12½) Very bright, small elliptical nucleus set in a large, faint, thickly elliptical halo. Pretty faint star (possibly H II region) noted N.W. of nucleus. Fainter H II region S.E. of nucleus; elliptical in shape.

Catalogue	R.A.	Dec.	mag.	Size	Type	Const.
NGC 2188	06 10.1	-34 05	12.5	3x0.6	ScdIII	Col

($12\frac{1}{2}$) Very long and thin with a very bright elongated nucleus, which is off-centre. A dark lane bisects the galaxy, which is brighter at its N. end. Small, extremely faint, almost round galaxy with a brighter centre is also in the field, 3' west.

NGC 2217	06 20.8	-27 15	12.0	4x3	SBa(s)	CMa

($12\frac{1}{2}$) A pretty bright, slightly oblate object (about 2' x 1'), with a very bright, very small (20") nucleus.

NGC 2283	06 45.9	-18 14	12.8	1x1	Sc	CMa

($16\frac{1}{2}$) An unusual object, more suggestive of a diffuse nebula than a galaxy. Quite faint, large and irregular in shape. At least 5 stars involved, of which 3 are easily seen.

NGC 2292	06 47.6	-26 45				CMa

($16\frac{1}{2}$) Elongated N.p.-S.f. At x176 shows a bright knot close to the end of the p. extension. NGC 2293 attached at S.f. end; round, small, brighter in the middle.

NGC 2295	06 47.3	-26 44	14.0			CMa

($16\frac{1}{2}$) Faintish object in a group of faint stars. Extended S.p.-N.f. and at x351 it is well seen, having a star located just beyond the ends of each extension. Brighter and wider in the centre. NGC 2295 lies p. NGC 2292/3.

Catalogue	R.A.	Dec.	mag.	Size	Type	Const.
NGC 2427	07 36.5	−47 36	12.4	5x3	Sc(s)II-III	Pup

($12\frac{1}{2}$) Very large but very faint and of even surface brightness. Elongated E-W, oblate. Extremely faint star immersed in N.W. edge.

NGC 2784	09 12.3	−24 10	12.0	3x1	SO1(4)	Hya

($12\frac{1}{2}$) Very bright elliptical object with a small, very bright elliptical core and a stellar nucleus.

NGC 2997	09 45.7	−31 12	10.5	6x5	Sc(s)I.3	Ant

($12\frac{1}{2}$) Extremely large, bright and easy. Elliptical in shape (about 6' x 4'.5). Very gradually brighter to a suddenly much brighter elliptical nucleus. Faint star at S. edge.

NGC 3001	09 46.3	−30 27	13.0	1.2x1.0	SBbc(s)I-II	Ant

($12\frac{1}{2}$) Almost round. Bright, with a stellar nucleus and a mag. 10 star at N. edge.

NGC 3109 DDO 236	10 03.0	−26 09	11.2	12x2	SmIV	Hya

(8) Very extended and thicker at the centre. Even brightness and texture. 2 stars seen in outer envelope.

The NGC 3271 Group of Galaxies.

Catalogue	R.A.	Dec.	mag.	Size	Type	Const.
NGC 3271	10 30.4	-35 21	12.9	1x0.6	Sa	Ant

Other members of this group include: NGC 3267 (Type E), NGC 3268 (Type E2), NGC 3269 (Type E) and IC 2585 (Type E).

($12\frac{1}{2}$) The NGC 3271 group of galaxies is a fine string of pretty faint elliptical-shaped nebulae running N.W.-S.E. and scattered over about 15'. The dominant object is NGC 3271.

NGC 3267: Very faint and slightly elongated, measuring 60" x 40". No nucleus noted. Most westerly member of the group, 2' p. NGC 3268.

NGC 3268: Faint, fairly large (80" x 40") and elongated N.W.-S.E. Even surface brightness. 3' N.p. NGC 3271.

NGC 3269: Faintest and smallest of the five objects seen. Round, with a gradually brighter centre. 30" diameter. E.f. star 30" E.

NGC 3271: Pretty bright elongated lens, about 80" x 30". Contains a much brighter elliptical nucleus. NGC 3271 lies 1'.5 N.N.W. of IC 2585.

IC 2585: Faint ellipse, elongated almost N.-S.; measures 60" x 25". No definite nucleus.

The NGC 3347 Group of Galaxies.

NGC 3347	10 42.7	-36 22	12.8	4x2	SBb(r)I	Ant

RNGC lists 3 anon. companions to NGC 3347.

($12\frac{1}{2}$) A fairly bright and easy group aligned W.N.W.-E.S.E.

NGC 3347: Pretty faint and elongated N.-S. Slightly brighter in the centre.

NGC 3354: Faint. Elongated. Even surface brightness. Mag. 14 star on N. edge

NGC 3358: Bright, round, with a much brighter small nucleus. Group of 5 stars of mags 10 - 12 just N.

Catalogue	R.A.	Dec.	mag.	Size	Type	Const.
NGC 3621	11 18.3 −32 48		10.6	5x2	Sc(s)II.8	Hya
	PKS 1115−325.					

(6) Large, dull, ill-defined nebula of even surface brightness. Slightly elongated in P.A. 190°.

NGC 3783	11 38.9 −37 44		13.0	1x0.9	SBa(r)I	Cen
	X-ray source A1136−37.					

(12$\frac{1}{2}$) Faint and round with a pretty bright stellar nucleus.

NGC 4594	12 39.9	−11 37	9.3	7x1.5	Sa^{+}/Sb^{-}	Vir
M.104						

(8$\frac{1}{2}$) At x77, clearly seen as an elongated streak, over 5' long, with a slightly brighter centre. At x116, the centre is more obviously brighter and seems to be offset slightly N. N. edge of galaxy seems almost straight but less well defined in nuclear bulge region.
(4$\frac{1}{4}$ RFT) At x42, seen as an elongated spindle with a brighter centre. Not very well defined. Contained in an interesting field including a line of bright stars, N.p., the one furthest from the galaxy being double (Σ1664).

NGC 4650	12 44.3	−40 43				Cen

(154) A remarkable elliptical galaxy with a large axial ratio of about 3:1. Across its shorter dimension, just away from the centre, runs a narrow dark lane. At great distances from the galaxy this is seen as a line of very faint nebulosity, with some locally brighter portions, out to several minutes of arc on either side. It appears as if there is a huge, almost edge-on, ring of material encircling the galaxy.

Catalogue	R.A.	Dec.	mag.	Size	Type	Const.
NGC 4945	13 05.3	−49 29	9.5	15x2.5	Sc	Cen

RNGC lists anon. companion. PKS 1302−49.

---

(6) Very large and bright. A much elongated lens with a much brighter elongated core. Situated in a rich starfield near a bright star.

NGC 5102	13 21.9	−36 39	10.8	6x2.5	S01(5)	Cen

---

(10) Fairly large and oblate with a well-defined much brighter oval core. An easy object; near *l* Cen.

NGC 5128	13 25.3	−43 01	7.5	10x8	S0+S pec.	Cen

Cen A. Arp 153. 4U 1322−42.

---

(154) Circular, diffuse galaxy crossed by an intricate dust lane. The detail in the dark lane is amazing and one small, faint knot is seen in it which is the nucleus of the galaxy itself, shining through the dust. Some distance from the galaxy are some very faint knots of nebulosity which lie on the axis of the double radio source: 4 seen.

($16\frac{1}{2}$) A large bright object, divided entirely across the centre by a wide dark lane. The southern half of the galaxy is brighter than the northern half. A star is located close to the N.p. edge of the band and within it.

(6) An extended area of haze surrounding an almost stellar centre. Dark lane not seen at x32 but apparent at x70 when the object appeared V-shaped.

Catalogue	R.A.	Dec.	mag.	Size	Type	Const
NGC 5236	13 37.1	−29 52	8.5	10x8	SBc(s)II	Hya
M.83	PKS 1334−29.	SN 1923A, 1950B, 1957D, 1968L, 1983				

(10) Large and bright with a much brighter, very condensed core, which is not quite stellar; it appears elliptical with 2 brighter extensions going N.W. and S.E. from the nucleus and involved in the larger, diffuse outer envelope. Definite mottling is seen throughout the envelope and with a.v. the tips of the bright extensions are curved slightly and quite short. 2 faint stars are at the tip of each arm.

(6) Very bright nucleus embedded in an extensive oval, diffuse nebula about 10' across. Two stars are seen within the nebula, one N. of the nucleus and the other S.E.

(12x40) Faint round spot with a brighter centre about 7° S. of the Mira variable R Hya.

Catalogue	R.A.	Dec.	mag.	Size	Type	Const
NGC 5253	13 39.9	−31 39	10.8	4x1.5	Amorphous	Cen
	Haro 10.	SN 1895B, 1972E.				

(10) Bright, with an extended envelope and small core.

The IC 4329 Group of Galaxies.

Catalogue	R.A.	Dec.	mag.	Size	Type	Const
IC 4329	13 49.0	−30 18	12.8	1.5x0.5	SO1(5)	Cen
	IC 4329 = 2A 1347−300.					

($12\frac{1}{2}$) The IC 4329 group is a very large aggregation of about 25 fairly faint galaxies, scattered over a region about 3° x 1°.5, with a concentrated area 20' x 18' containing 9 of the brighter members in a rich star field. Among the galaxies observed in this group are the following, which are identified on the chart at the rear of this section:

1. IC 4329: At x145, very bright and easy. Lies in the N.E. of the group, closely followed by MCG 05−33−019. Pretty large and lenticular in form, with a bright core and a very small brighter nucleus. Elongated E − W, 60" x 30".

The IC 4329 Group of Galaxies (cont'd).

2. MCG 05-33-019: Some 90" N.f. IC 4329, this object is pretty small and pretty bright. Almost round - possibly elongated E.N.E. - W.S.W. Contains a pretty bright core. About 20" x 15".

3. NGC 5304: Bright, elliptical galaxy, brighter in the centre. Elongated N - S with a mag. 11 star very close at the N.f. end. Measures about 40" x 25".

4. MCG 05-33-015: Using x145, pretty bright and elliptical in shape, with a bright core. Elongated N.N.E. - S.S.W. and measures 30" x 50". IC 4329 is 5' N.f. and NGC 5298 is 4' p. Mag. 14.5.

5. NGC 5298: Small, round and pretty bright, in a field E. and slightly N. of NGC 5291. Bright core. May be slightly elongated N.E. - S.W. Measures 30" across. Surrounded E., W. & N. by 4 pretty faint stars.

6. NGC 5302: Faint and pretty small ellipse, containing a bright centre, about 30" x 45". Elongated N - S. Lies 1' f. a mag. 13 star.

7. Anon.: An extremely faint, small, elliptical object N.f. the much easier MCG 05-33-014 and 2' S. of a bright field star. Est. mag. 16.0.

8. MCG 05-33-011: Faint and small and containing a much brighter elongated core. Elongated N - S, size about 50" x 30". Closely f. and p. are 2 extremely faint stars.

9. MCG 05-33-009: Very faint and round with a slightly brighter centre. Small, 30" diameter. Preceding of 3, being followed immediately by No. 8 and at a greater distance by No. 7.

Not shown on the chart are the following NGC & IC objects: NGC 5291, NGC 5292, IC 4319, IC 4321, IC 4324, IC 4327 and IC 4328.

Catalogue	R.A.	Dec.	mag.	Size	Type	Const
NGC 5530	14 18.5	−43 23	12.3	3.5x2.0	Sc(s)II.8	Lup

(10) Fairly large but thin oval with a much brighter, almost stellar, nucleus.

Catalogue	R.A.	Dec.	mag.	Size	Type	Const
AP Librae	15 17.5	−24 23	14.5-16.0		BL Lac	Lib

(40) Decidedly non-stellar, the bright nucleus fading out into a diffuse haze 30" in diameter, very like an elliptical galaxy. Stellar centre. Mag. approx. 14.5.

Catalogue	R.A.	Dec.	mag.	Size	Type	Const
NGC 6215	16 51.1	−59 01	11.2	1.7x1.3	Sc(s)II	Ara

RNGC lists anon. companion. η Arae 80" W.

(40) A fairly subdued object but with a clearly visible spiral pattern. Nuclear region round and diffuse with a faint nucleus. From one side of this region a fairly conspicuous arm emerges and winds about 90° before it is lost in the glow of the disc. Fainter arc on opposite side suspected. No distinct knots visible.

Catalogue	R.A.	Dec.	mag.	Size	Type	Const
NGC 6221	16 52.9	−59 12	11.4	2.7x2.0	Sbc(s)II-III	Ara

(40) Forms a wide pair with NGC 6215. A less clearly organised system consisting of a conspicuous nucleus crossed by an arc of nebulosity which extends into a broad diffuse arm. A detached zone of much fainter nebulosity is visible on the opposite side of the galaxy. One bright knot visible, just off one end of the arc crossing the nucleus. Star field very rich.

Catalogue	R.A.	Dec.	mag.	Size	Type	Const
NGC 6300	17 16.8	−62 50	11.4	3.9x3.5	SBb(s)IIpec	Ara

----

(40) A ring surrounding a bar, though seen with some difficulty. At x520 the ring is clear on one side but is subtle and shows no details. The bar is less conspicuous on one side.

NGC 6438 &	18 25.8	−85 25	12.4			Oct
NGC 6438A						

----

(40) Two fairly small and fairly faint galaxies essentially in contact. One is very compact and only barely distinguishable from a star. The other, very diffuse, arches slightly around the compact one.

NGC 6744	19 09.6	−63 52	10.0	9x9	Sbc(r)II	Pav

----

(158) This galaxy greatly overflows the field of view. There is a very bright, broad bar with a bright centre. Near one side of the bar is a faint, very thin luminous arc. No other structure observed.

NGC 6769–	19 18.3	−60 29	12.7	2x1.2	SBb	Pav
70–71						

Mag./Size/Type applies to NGC 6769. NGC 6770 & 6771 are of Type S. VV 304.

----

(40) A group of three conspicuous galaxies. Two are round and diffuse and the third, slightly away from the other two, is slightly elongated with a faint nucleus. Many stars in field.

Catalogue	R.A.	Dec.	mag.	Size	Type	Const
NGC 6822	19 44.9	−14 45	11.0	20x10	ImIV-V	Sgr

Local Group. Incl. 16 HII regions, the brightest being IC 1308 & IC 4895. Brightest stars, mag. 15. DDO 209.

(12½) Very large and very faint, LSB object. Even surface brightness. A few stars noted around the edges. Three emission nebulae have also been seen associated with the galaxy: Hubble I – the brightest, but even so, only of about mag. 13.5. Round, about 30" diam. Hubble V – very faint and slightly oblate. N. edge brightest. Hubble X – v. small (about 25" x 10") and of about mag. 14. Elongated N.W. – S.E. Faint star S.f. Hubble III, which forms a pair with Hubble I, not seen.
(8½) Difficult due to low altitude. At x51 appears as a barely discernable nebulous patch extended N – S. At x102, still very faint but seems comprised of 3 distinct but connected regions. No indications of the 2 IC nebulae which, although not extremely faint, are quite small.

The NGC 7172 Group of Galaxies

NGC 7172	22 01.9	−31 53	12.9	1.6x0.6	Sa	PsA

Includes NGC 7173-4-6, all Type E, mag. 12.9 – 13.2.

----

(10) An attractive and very close trio of pretty bright galaxies with a fourth member (7172) about 12' N.f.

NGC 7172: A bright lenticular system of even surface brightness, orientated S.p. – N.f., measuring about 90" x 30". Mag. 11 star 2' N.

NGC 7173: Small, pretty bright and of even surface brightness. Orientated N.p. – S.f. 1' N.p. 7174.

NGC 7174: Faintest of trio. Round and small.

NGC 7176: Brightest and most southerly of trio, slightly elongated N.E. – S.W. Bright nucleus. Size 50" x 40". Lies 1' S. of 7173.

Catalogue	R.A.	Dec.	mag.	Size	Type	Const
NGC 7204	22 06.9	−31 08	14.0			PsA

(40) Not especially conspicuous. Has three distinct knots connected by faint nebulosity.

Catalogue	R.A.	Dec.	mag.	Size	Type	Const
NGC 7314	22 35.8	−26 02	11.9	3.5x3.5	Sc(s)III	PsA

(12½) Large and bright. A lens-shaped and elongated system with no dominant core or nucleus visible, however, very gradually brighter to the centre. E.f. stars noted W. of northern end of galaxy.

Catalogue	R.A.	Dec.	mag.	Size	Type	Const
NGC 7412	22 55.8	−42 39	12.2	3x2	Sc(rs)I-II	Gru

(10) Faint, pretty large and thickly elliptical, with a box-like appearance. No nucleus noted. Even surface brightness. A bright (mag. 6) star interferes with observations.

Catalogue	R.A.	Dec.	mag.	Size	Type	Const
NGC 7424	22 57.3	−41 04	11.0	6x6	Sc(s)II.8	Gru

(40) An exceptionally diffuse, broad bar visible at x500. Contrast so poor that the faint disc of this large spiral not seen.

Catalogue	R.A.	Dec.	mag.	Size	Type	Const
NGC 7496	23 09.8	−43 26	12.0	2x1	SBc(s)II.8	Gru

(40) Appears to be a barred spiral. Structure is quite subtle but contrast is poor due to high magnification. Curved bar suspected with a knot on one end and a broad, diffuse twist on the other end which turned 180° and possibly returned close to the bar on its opposite side. Faint nucleus visible in centre of bar.

NGC 7531	23 14.9	−43 37	12.0	1.5x0.5	Sbc(r)I-II	Gru

(158) Small bulge situated in a very bright lens, at the rim of which there is a conspicuous ring. Beyond this ring is a very low surface brightness disc which appears narrow and curved.
(24) Nucleus visible within an elongated lens but no other structure visible.

NGC 7702	23 35.5	−56 01	13.1	1.3x1.0	RSa(r)	Phe

(158) Very remarkable! A beautiful galaxy resembling the planet Saturn. Bright bulge surrounded by an extremely bright, smooth elliptical ring which is slightly enhanced in the regions near the major axis. The ring is broad and inside it are irregularities in the light distribution which suggests the presence of dust.
(36) Still beautiful and distinctive but ring now only suspected.

Catalogue	R.A.	Dec.	mag.	Size	Type	Const
NGC 7713	23 36.5	-37 57	12.0		Sc(s)II-III	Scl

RNGC lists anon. companion. SN 1982

----

(40) Very bright, extended, mottled. No clear knots. Quite diffuse and large.

NGC 7793	23 57.9	-32 35	9.7	6x4	Sd(s)IV	Scl

Sculptor Group.

($12\frac{1}{2}$) Very large, bright oval galaxy with a much brighter elliptical nucleus, possibly off-centre. Mag. 11 star at N.f. edge.

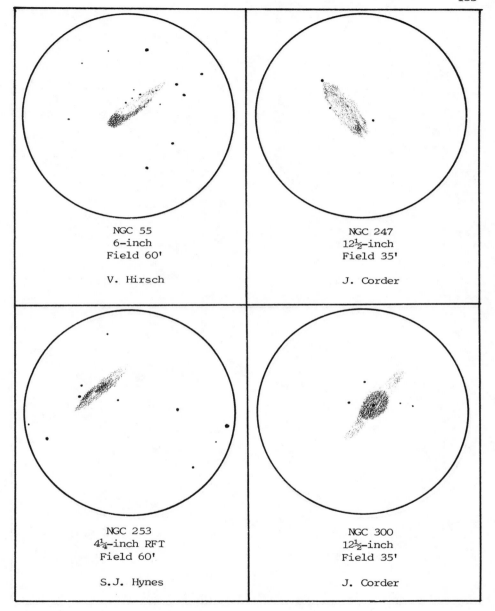

NGC 55
6-inch
Field 60'

V. Hirsch

NGC 247
12½-inch
Field 35'

J. Corder

NGC 253
4¼-inch RFT
Field 60'

S.J. Hynes

NGC 300
12½-inch
Field 35'

J. Corder

136

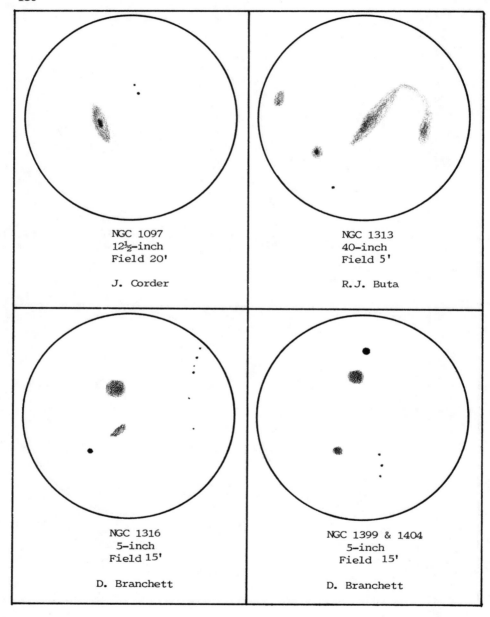

NGC 1097
12½-inch
Field 20'

J. Corder

NGC 1313
40-inch
Field 5'

R.J. Buta

NGC 1316
5-inch
Field 15'

D. Branchett

NGC 1399 & 1404
5-inch
Field 15'

D. Branchett

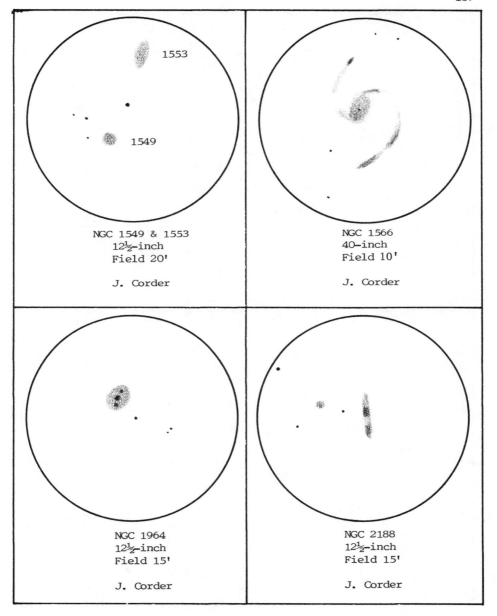

137

NGC 1549 & 1553
12½-inch
Field 20'

J. Corder

NGC 1566
40-inch
Field 10'

J. Corder

NGC 1964
12½-inch
Field 15'

J. Corder

NGC 2188
12½-inch
Field 15'

J. Corder

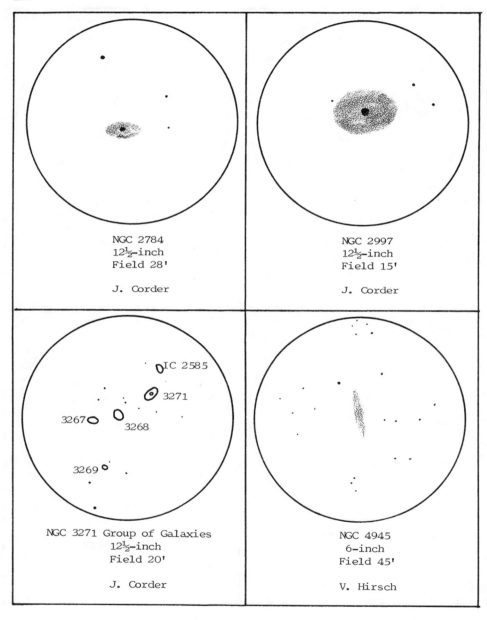

NGC 2784
12½-inch
Field 28'

J. Corder

NGC 2997
12½-inch
Field 15'

J. Corder

IC 2585
3271
3267
3268
3269

NGC 3271 Group of Galaxies
12½-inch
Field 20'

J. Corder

NGC 4945
6-inch
Field 45'

V. Hirsch

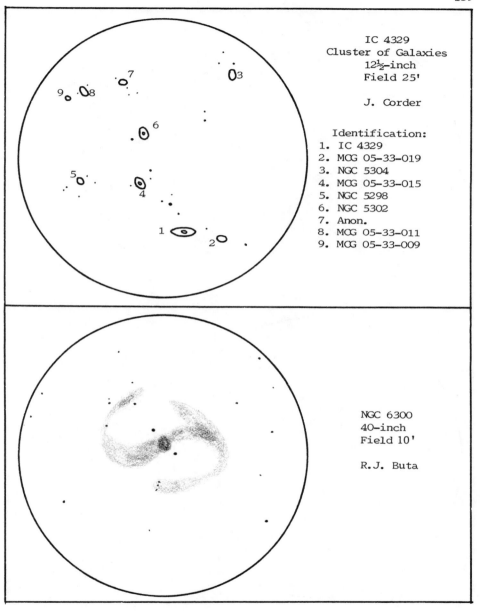

IC 4329
Cluster of Galaxies
12½-inch
Field 25'

J. Corder

Identification:
1. IC 4329
2. MCG 05-33-019
3. NGC 5304
4. MCG 05-33-015
5. NGC 5298
6. NGC 5302
7. Anon.
8. MCG 05-33-011
9. MCG 05-33-009

NGC 6300
40-inch
Field 10'

R.J. Buta

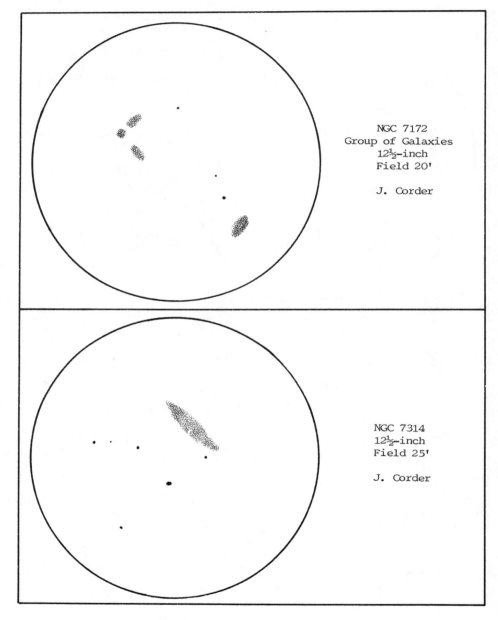

NGC 7172
Group of Galaxies
12½-inch
Field 20'

J. Corder

NGC 7314
12½-inch
Field 25'

J. Corder

Catalogue

SECTION 6: THE MAGELLANIC CLOUDS

Data provided with this section:

(a) R.A. and Dec. for Epoch 2000.0
(b) Apparent magnitude
(c) Size (in degrees)
(d) Type
(e) Constellation

The data in (b) and (c) is taken from Burnham's Celestial Handbook (Burnham, 1978). The data in (d) is taken from the Revised Shapley-Ames Catalogue of Galaxies (Sandage & Tammann, 1981).

Observers and Accredited Objects

LMC:

Naked-eye – CH
12x40 bin. – CH

NGC 1714	– RJB	NGC 1910	– DAA, RJB, VH
1755	– RJB	1929-34-5-6	– RJB, VH
1761-63-69	– RJB, VH	1978	– RJB
1783	– RJB	1994	– DAA
1818	– RJB	2004	– DAA, RJB, VH
1831	– RJB	2029-32-35	– RJB
1850	– DAA, RJB	2040	– RJB
1854-5	– DAA	2057	– VH
1856	– RJB	2070	– RJB, VH
1860	– DAA	2100	– RJB
1903	– DAA, RJB		

SMC:

Naked-eye – CH
12x40 bin. – CH

NGC 121	– RJB	NGC 371	– RJB
220-2	– RJB	376	– RJB
249-61	– RJB	419	– RJB
330	– RJB	456	– RJB
346	– RJB		

The Large Magellanic Cloud (LMC)

R.A.	Dec.	mag.	Size	Type	Const.
05 23.7	-69 05	0.6	6°	SBmIII	Dor/Men

Local Group; satellite of Milky Way. See Part 2 for details.

(N.E.) the main bar of the galaxy is easily seen, together with
projections from the ends of the bar which extend N.p. and S.f. The N.p.
projection includes the 30 Doradus nebula at its tip. An extensive, but
tenuous nebulosity is apparent to the N. of the bar, and this includes a
brighter condensation which is the complex involving NGC 1974 & 1955.
Compared with the Carina star cloud, the central condensation within the
main bar is marginally brighter, making the LMC a very bright object
indeed.

(12x40) the structure of the LMC is very complicated and many individual
features can be identified. Feature A is an arc shaped nebulosity,
brighter towards the following end. Feature B is an isolated nebulous
spot; located within it are three small condensations, which may possibly
be faint stars. Features C and D are the brighter portions of a detached
fragment, possibly part of one of the spiral arms. Feature E, connected
to the main bar, points towards it and is also visible when observing
with the naked-eye. This structure is represented at the other end of
the bar by feature H, which points in the opposite direction, however, it
is very faint.   The 30 Doradus nebula is the brightest part of feature F;
here, there are five bright patches of nebulosity, of which three appear
detached from the main bar. The 30 Doradus nebula is located at the f.
end of one of these patches and is separated from its nearest neighbour
by what is probably a dark lane of obscuring matter. The appearance of
30 Doradus itself is very similar to that of a bright globular cluster,
being round, brighter in the centre and fading towards the periphery;
12x40 binoculars do not reveal any of the spider-like filaments which
can be seen telescopically. Feature G is the brightest portion of the
main bar and is otherwise structureless. Nebulous spots can be seen at
various locations in and around the LMC.

Objects within the LMC

NGC 1714 (Diffuse Nebula):
(24) Beautiful high surface brightness nebula. Has a quadrilateral
appearance with a star embedded on one of the sides. Very small but
stands magnification well. A particularly interesting object.

143

The Large Magellanic Cloud (cont'd).

NGC 1755 (Globular Cluster):
(30) Very bright globular in a poor starfield. Slightly oval and
mottled but only a few stars possibly resolved.

NGC 1761-63-69 (Nebula and star cluster complex):
(24) A remarkable region. NGC 1763 is a very bright, elongated nebula
showing definite structural details and which appears to envelope a
bright open cluster. NGC 1769 is also spectacular, but does not include
a cluster. Instead, it has a single bright star near the centre, which
is crossed by a curved band of nebulosity. The structure to either side
of the band makes the object butterfly-shaped. NGC 1761 is a large open
cluster to the W. of the two nebulae. Starfield very rich.
(6) A striking object, giving the impression of a nebulous ring, broken
in several places. Three sections distinctly seen. Only one star noted,
embedded in the S.W. section of the ring. NGC 1761 visible as a hazy
spot roughly S. of the nebulae.

NGC 1783 (Globular Cluster):
(30) Very bright globular in poor starfield. Large and diffuse but not
resolved.

NGC 1818 (Globular cluster):
(30) Beautiful, round and very bright cluster. Fairly compact and only
partly resolved.

NGC 1831 (Globular Cluster):
(30) Very large and exceptionally diffuse globular cluster in a poor
starfield. Unresolved and shows only the slightest central condensation.

NGC 1850 (Nebulous Cluster):
(40) About 100 stars in a cluster 3' in diameter.
(30) Bright object made of two oval components, neither of which appeared
to be unresolved clusters. The southern component is brightest and
slightly enhanced at its centre; it has fairly high surface brightness.
The northern component appears more elongated and includes at least one
faint star. The two objects are surrounded by many stars.

NGC 1854-5 (Open cluster):
(40) Seen as a single cluster 2' across. 50 stars noted, possibly some
nebulosity.

NGC 1856 (Globular Cluster):
(24) Fine globular in an extremely poor starfield. Very bright, mottled
and fairly well concentrated. Only one faint star suspected.

The Large Magellanic Cloud (cont'd)

NGC 1860 (Open Cluster):
(40) Appears as a nebula about 1' across; slightly elongated N-S. Seen
in the same field of view as NGC 1850, 1854-5, 1858 and HS 152.

NGC 1903 (Open Cluster):
(40) Bright nebula, 25" x 20", elongated in P.A. 110° - 290°.
(24) Bright but completely unresolved. NGC 1916,which is of a similar
nature and appearance, is in the same x300 field. Both are set in a
beautiful starfield.

NGC 1910 (Nebulous Cluster):
(40) Rather loose group of 20 stars in a faint nebula.
(24) Large, very bright open cluster in a rich starfield. Fills the
whole field of view at x300. Patchy zones of faint nebulosity suspected
in various places.
(6) One of five distinct little nebulous patches in a very rich 32' field.
NGC 1910 appeared as a small fan-shaped nebula with a star at its S.W.
edge.

NGC 1929-34-35-36 (Nebulous Clusters):
(30) A very interesting region. The field includes 4 very bright
nebulous objects strung in a line N.W. to S.E. NGC 1929 appears compact
with a conspicuous central condensation and is the smallest of the four.
NGC 1934 appears large and diffuse and has a conspicuous star on W. edge.
NGC 1935 is round and diffuse and includes several stars. NGC 1936 is
most interesting as it not only includes a very bright, round part, but
also a fainter and very extensive wisp which arcs towards NGC 1935. The
starfield due S. of these objects is much richer than that to the N. and
could be a very large extended open cluster.
(6) An ill-defined nebulous area with a more concentrated centre. Not
resolved. With NGC 1936 at the centre of a 32' field there is a bright
star almost due N., near the edge of the field. The space between is
spangled with tiny stars.

NGC 1978 (Globular Cluster):
(24) A large, bright globular, but diffuse and unresolved. Slightly oval
shape. Starfield moderately rich.

NGC 1994 (Open Cluster):
(40) 30 stars in a compact group 15" in diameter.

NGC 2004 (Globular Cluster (?)):
(40) About 100 stars in a cluster 30" in diameter. Not fully resolved.
(30) Compact and apparently resolved. Small, round, diffuse core
surrounded by many faint stars as if only outer parts are resolvable.

The Large Magellanic Cloud (cont'd)

NGC 2004 (cont'd)
(6) Faint nebulous spot, with some slight resolution suspected.

NGC 2029-32-35 (Diffuse Nebulae):
(30) A remarkable field. NGC 2032 and 2035 are bright and contain much
structure. NGC 2032 is very extended N-S and is fan-shaped. In its
brightest part it arcs slightly towards NGC 2035 and includes a few very
faint stars. NGC 2035 is irregular in outline (perhaps a little like a
cross) and also includes a few very faint stars. NGC 2029 is a much
fainter but definite extended glow close to W. of NGC 2032-35. No visible
stars noted. NGC 2040 close by.

NGC 2040 (Nebulous Cluster):
(30) Compact nebulous object to N.E. of NGC 2029-32-35 complex. Several
stars involved, may be a partly resolved cluster.

NGC 2057 (Open Cluster):
(6) Very faint star cloud.

NGC 2070 (Diffuse Nebula):
(36) Absolutely incredible! At x500 it is seen as an extremely
complicated nebula of very high surface brightness. The central section
is exceptionally distinct and shows a ribbon-like structure with one
particularly conspicuous loop. In this section is a cluster of stars
consisting of one bright star surrounded by many faint ones. Several
conspicuous, long streaks of nebulosity near the central section arc
toward a second, poorer cluster.
(16) Looped structure in the central section is clearly visible;
extensive regions of nebulosity seen beyond the central loops. The
cluster can be seen but is very faint.
(2¼ O.G.) Bright nebula showing structure like a clenched fist or
convoluted brain. A number of stars are superimposed.

NGC 2100 (Open Cluster):
(30) Very fine! An extremely bright and well resolved cluster that
includes a faint underlying diffuse glow. In none of the other compact
clusters have so many stars been resolved. NGC 2092 noted as an
extended glow due W. of NGC 2100.

....

The Small Magellanic Cloud (SMC)

R.A.	Dec.	mag.	Size	Type	Const.
00 52.7	-72 50	1.5	$3\frac{1}{2}^{\circ}$	Im IV-V	Tuc

Local Group; satellite of Milky Way. See Part 2 for details.

(N.E.) The SMC is comma-shaped, with the brightest and widest section located near the southern end. At the tip of the comma is a small, hazy spot and located nearby is the globular cluster 47 Tucanae (NGC 104), also easily visible to the naked-eye.

(12x40) The 'comma' appearance remains apparent and on the following side of this a faint, ill-defined glow is evident. At the northern end of the SMC at least 5 small nebulous spots can be identified. The general body of the SMC is otherwise featureless.

Objects within the SMC

NGC 121 (Globular Cluster):
(40) Very bright but mostly unresolved.

NGC 220-2 (Open Clusters):
(40) Two clusters close together. Both appear round and mostly unresolved. Starfield quite rich. NGC 220 is brighter than NGC 222.

NGC 249-61 (Diffuse Nebulae):
(40) Two diffuse nebulae in the same x200 field of view. NGC 249 is small and round, while NGC 261 appears larger, diffuse and includes a central star. There is a weak spot in the nebula just S. of this star. Lies in a rich starfield.

NGC 330 (Globular Cluster):
(40) About a dozen stars seen near the centre, overlying a distinct unresolved glow that is slightly elongated. Starfield very rich.

NGC 346 (Nebulous Cluster):
(40) An elongated cluster enveloped in extensive nebulosity that fills most of the field at x520. About two dozen stars seen. The nebula is visible around the cluster, forming arcs at each end, giving the appearance of a barred spiral galaxy. There is a small, nearly stellar, nebula or cluster near the end of one of the arcs.

The Small Magellanic Cloud (cont'd)

NGC 371 (Nebulous Cluster):
(30) A very large cluster which fills the whole field of view with
faint stars. Shows no central condensation. Both NGC 371 and nearby
NGC 346 can be seen with binoculars.

NGC 376 (Open Cluster):
(24) At low magnification, this small cluster is very pretty and bright.
About a dozen stars resolved at x300, but more would probably be visible
with better sky conditions. Cluster seemed completely resolved.

NGC 419 (Globular Cluster):
(40) A bright, large and diffuse object but not resolved, however, it was
observed under moonlight conditions.

NGC 456 (Nebulous Cluster):
(24) Large nebula of fairly low surface brightness, in a moderately rich
star field. The nebula is oval and on S. edge is an elongated, mottled
condensation which appears to be a partly resolved cluster. Two other
objects are visible in the same field: NGC 460, a much fainter and
smaller diffuse nebulous object to the S.E., and a nearly stellar
nebulous object almost due E. A very fine region.

....

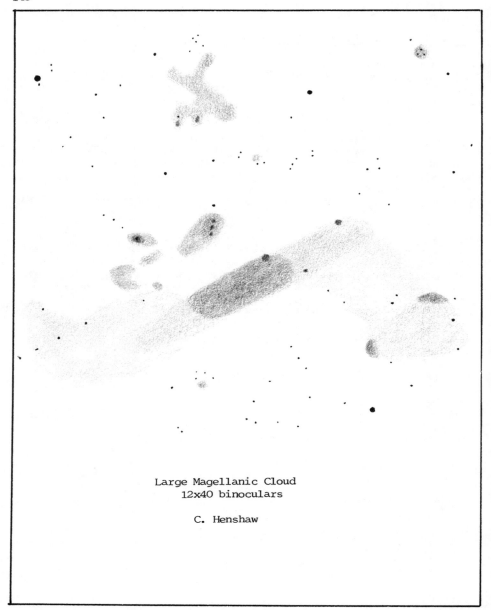

Large Magellanic Cloud
12x40 binoculars

C. Henshaw

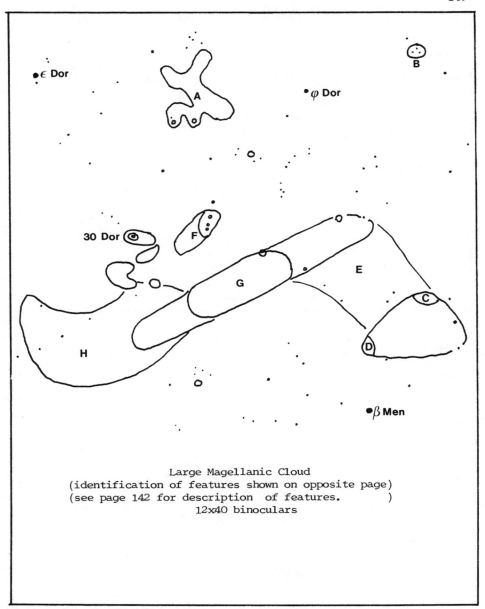

Large Magellanic Cloud
(identification of features shown on opposite page)
(see page 142 for description of features.   )
12x40 binoculars

NGC 1714
24-inch

R.J. Buta

NGC 1763
24-inch

R.J. Buta

NGC 1818
30-inch

R.J. Buta

NGC 1850
30-inch

R.J. Buta

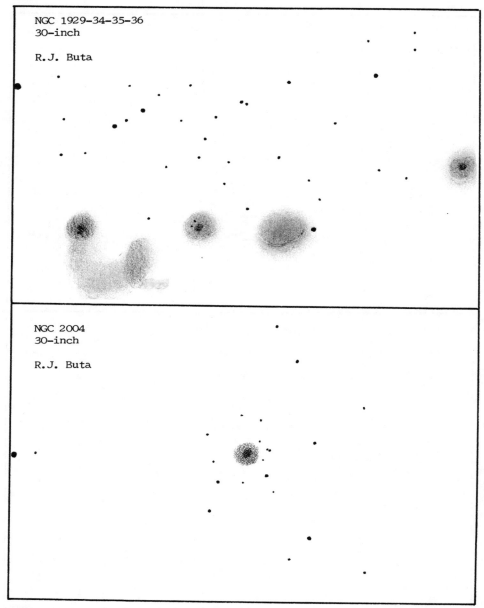

NGC 1929-34-35-36
30-inch

R.J. Buta

NGC 2004
30-inch

R.J. Buta

153

NGC 2032-5
30-inch

R.J. Buta

NGC 2100
30-inch

R.J. Buta

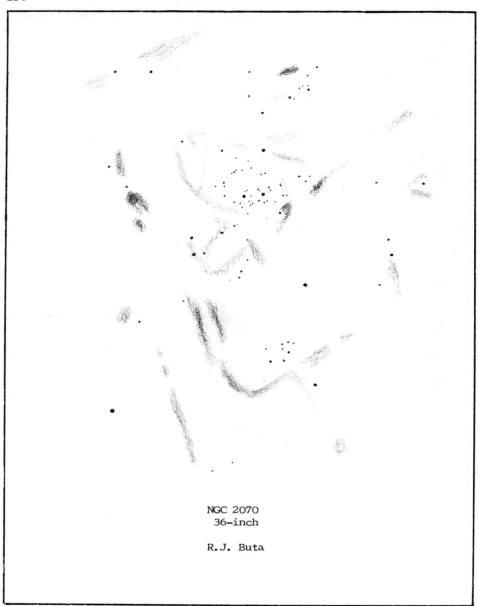

NGC 2070
36-inch

R.J. Buta

NGC 121
40-inch

R.J. Buta

NGC 220-2
40-inch

R.J. Buta

156

NGC 249 & 261
40-inch

R.J. Buta

NGC 376
24-inch

R.J. Buta

NGC 456
24-inch

R.J. Buta

NGC 419
24-inch

R.J. Buta

PART FOUR

APPENDICES

159

Appendices

APPENDIX 1: TRAVELLING WITH A TELESCOPE.

International air transport and package holidays being comparatively
inexpensive these days, many readers will no doubt have some experience
of foreign travel. This gives the amateur astronomer the opportunity to
observe different regions of the heavens not previously experienced, but
how many actually take equipment to make the best of this? For
'northerners', the southern skies offer many splendid sights, some of
which are described in this volume, including, for example, the starfields
of Sagittarius and Scorpius, the Magellanic Clouds, the η Carinae nebula
and omega Centauri.

Of course, there can be some problems in transporting astronomical
equipment, but with a little thought and planning, the rewards certainly
compensate for any effort. In recent years my 10.5 cm. Edmund Astroscan
RFT has accompanied me on trips to Sri Lanka, Tenerife and Crete without
mishap and I have found the following guidelines worth following to
reduce the likelihood of encountering any difficulties.

First of all however, some advance research is required so that the
observer will have an idea of the geographical and meteorological
conditions likely to prevail at the destination. This may have a bearing
on the timing of the trip or choice of base in the destination country,
for example. In particular, check the following points: is there a
monsoon or 'rainy season'? Is there any other climatic peculiarity (such
as large amounts of sand suspended in the atmosphere at particular times
of year)? Are there any large hills or mountains close by and in what
direction? Is your intended base in a forested region? Are the lights
of nearby towns likely to interfere with observations? In resolving
these queries, embassies and national tourist offices are often pleased
to provide free information, brochures and maps. Travel agents and local
libraries can also be a good source of facts and figures.

For the deep-sky observer another important point is to find out the
phase of the Moon during your intended stay!

The next consideration must be to check customs and travel formalties.
As a precautionary measure it is worth checking with Embassies or High
Commissions whether any particular import regulations apply in the
country concerned. For short stays there are not usually any problems
here but if in doubt send them full details of the equipment you propose
to take and get a written reply to your enquiry, which you should take

160

Appendices

with you when you travel. Needless to say, you should also take any documents you have relating to the purchase of your telescope, binoculars or photographic equipment.

Since astronomical equipment tends to be of rather delicate construction you may want to take it as hand luggage if travelling by air. Check with a travel agent the current regulations relating to the size and nature of objects which may be taken as hand luggage in relation to the particular destination (it is worth noting that for many destinations the _weight_ of your hand luggage does not count towards your baggage allowance). In the absence of a compact telescope, binoculars are also worth taking for astronomical purposes but of course, unlike many of the compact telescopes available which have table-top cradles or tripods, binoculars really need a tall, sturdy tripod for effective use as an astronomical instrument. Ensure that your tripod is not only sufficiently rigid but can also be dismantled to the extent required to be taken as part of your holiday luggage.

Finally, here is a check-list of the basic requirements for the 'tourist astronomer':

1. Instrument - either binoculars plus tripod or compact telescope.

2. Holdall - it may seem unnecessary to include this but I do so for two reasons: (a) a telescope carried on its own may get accidentally knocked and damaged but in a holdall could easily be protected by padding, e.g., a beach towel. (b) with some countries being excessively security conscious, it is sometimes wise not to attract too much attention. A hard metallic case or unfamiliar piece of equipment of uncertain purpose might be a cause of problems, particularly if there are also language difficulties!

3. Star Atlas - nothing too bulky required and one which identifies the type of object by some kind of colour code is useful. 'Atlas Coeli' or Tirion's 'Sky Atlas 2000.0' are good choices.

4. Catalogue of objects - most standard catalogues tend to be large and heavy and I would therefore recommend making your own list, with notes about the size and approximate brightness of objects. Obviously, be realistic and take into account the limitations of your particular instrument.

5. Notepaper, pencils and pens.

Appendices

6. Torch – remember to take spare batteries, they inevitably fail at the most inconvenient time and when it is impossible to obtain replacements!

   The above should cover most eventualities but readers will doubtless think of other items which would also be useful.

Appendices

APPENDIX 2: OBSERVING THE LARGE MAGELLANIC CLOUD.

The LMC, which has been described in Part 2 of this Volume, is a treasurehouse of observational material for both amateur and professional observers. Indeed, the NGC alone includes 318 LMC objects (representing just over 4% of the total number of objects recorded in that catalogue); many more nebulae and clusters are also to be found in the IC and more recent catalogues. As a result of the richness of this region the observer is often left with the problem of identifying individual objects when several may appear in the same field of view. The problem is made worse by the effect of the distance of the LMC, which causes even bright LMC open and globular clusters to appear as irresolvable nebulous spots in smaller amateur instruments.

To aid the observer this Appendix contains six charts covering much of the area of the LMC and identifying many of the major objects in these areas, as well as a good number of fainter objects which could only be picked up using larger instruments. In addition, a more general contour diagram of the LMC is given, identifying just a few objects, so that the observer can relate to which areas of the LMC the more detailed charts apply.

The charts are based on those by Hodge and Wright (1967) and an examination of the ESO print ESO(B)056, taken with the ESO 1.0 m. Schmidt and kindly provided by Kurt Kjär.

Objects shown on the charts are identified by the following code:

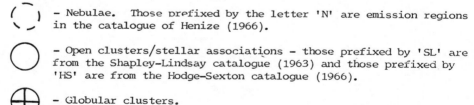

( ) - Nebulae. Those prefixed by the letter 'N' are emission regions in the catalogue of Henize (1966).

◯ - Open clusters/stellar associations - those prefixed by 'SL' are from the Shapley-Lindsay catalogue (1963) and those prefixed by 'HS' are from the Hodge-Sexton catalogue (1966).

⊕ - Globular clusters.

Four-figure numbers, with no prefix, are objects listed in Dreyer's New General Catalogue (1888). IC objects are identified as such.

Appendices

Each of the detailed charts is approximately 70' x 50' in size, with North at the top.

As a further aid to the observer, some of the more prominent LMC objects are listed below, together with their positions for Epoch 2000.0:

NGC	R.A.	Dec.	mag.	Type	Notes
1755	04 55.0	−68 11	9.9	OCl.	
1770	04 57.0	−68 24	9.0	Neb. OCl.	
1786	04 59.1	−67 45	10.1	GCl.	
1814	05 03.8	−67 17	9.0	Neb. OCl.	
1818	05 04.2	−66 24	9.8	OCl.	
1835	05 05.2	−69 24	9.8	GCl.	
1848	05 07.3	−71 11		Neb. OCl.	
1850	05 08.5	−68 46	9.4	Neb. OCl.	N.103
1856	05 09.3	−69 08		OCl.	
1866	05 13.5	−65 28	9.9	OCl.	
1871	05 13.6	−67 29		Neb. OCl.	
1873	05 13.6	−67 21		Neb. OCl.	
1874	05 13.3	−69 24		Neb. OCl.	
1910	05 18.1	−69 13		OCl.	S Dor involved
1929–34–36	05 21.6	−67 55		OB assoc. + neb.	
1937	05 22.4	−67 54		Neb. OCl.	
1948	05 25.6	−66 14		Neb. OCl.	
1955	05 26.0	−67 29		Neb. OCl.	N.51
1962	05 26.4	−68 47	8.5	Neb. OCl.	
1966	05 26.8	−68 49	8.5	Neb. OCl.	
1968	05 27.1	−67 26	9.0	Neb. OCl.	N.51
1974	05 27.8	−67 24	9.0	Neb. OCl.	N.51
1978	05 28.5	−66 14	9.9	GCl.	
1984	05 27.6	−69 06		Neb. OCl.	
2001	05 29.0	−68 44	9.8	OCl.	
2004	05 30.6	−67 17	10.0	OCl.	
2014	05 32.3	−67 40	8.5	Neb. OCl.	
2018	05 30.6	−71 04		Neb.	SNR involved
2021	05 33.5	−67 26		Neb. OCl.	
2031	05 33.6	−70 59		OCl.	
2033	05 34.5	−69 44		Neb. OCl.	2037 adjacent
2048	05 35.2	−69 46		Neb. OCl.	
2070	05 39.6	−69 03		Neb.	= Tarantula Neb.
2074–81	05 39.6	−69 27		Neb. OCl.	N.158
2078–83–4	05 39.9	−69 46		Neb. OCl.	N.159. 2079 adj.

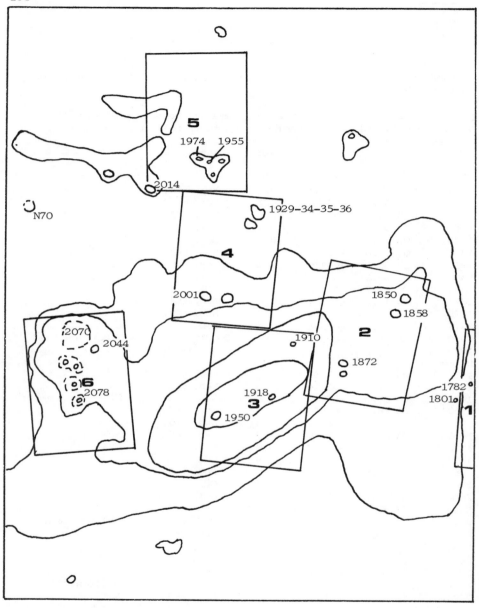

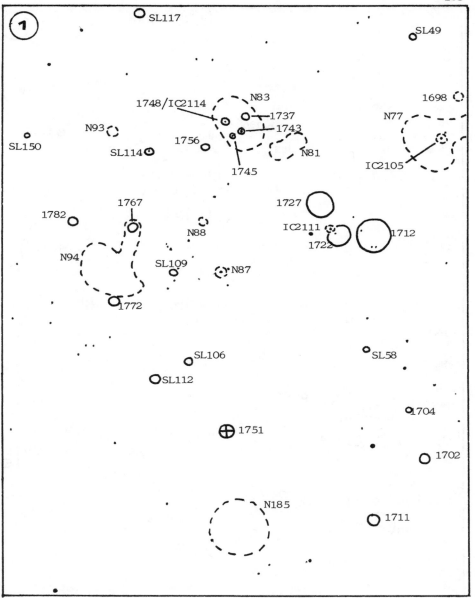

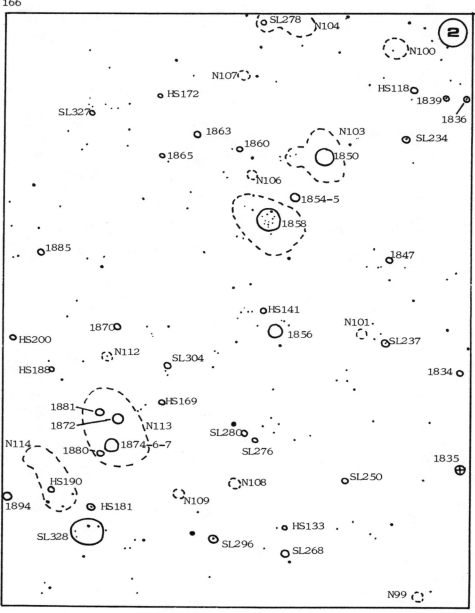

SL278
N104
N100
N107
HS172
HS118
1839
1836
SL327
1863
N103
1865
1860
1850
SL234
N106
1854-5
1858
1885
1847
HS141
N101
1870
1856
SL237
HS200
N112
1834
HS188
SL304
1881
HS169
1872
N113
SL280
N114
1880
1874-6-7
SL276
1835
HS190
SL250
1894
HS181
N108
N109
SL328
HS133
SL296
SL268
N99

2

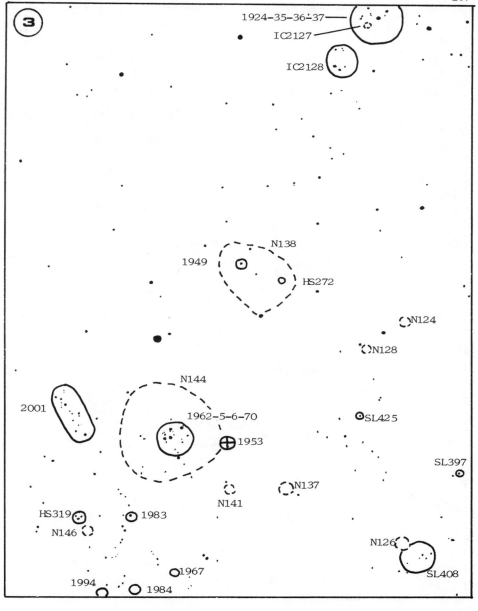

③

1924-35-36-37 ——
IC2127
IC2128

N138
1949
HS272

N124
N128

N144
2001
1962-5-6-70
1953
SL425
SL397

N137
N141
HS319 1983
N146
N126
SL408

1967
1994 1984

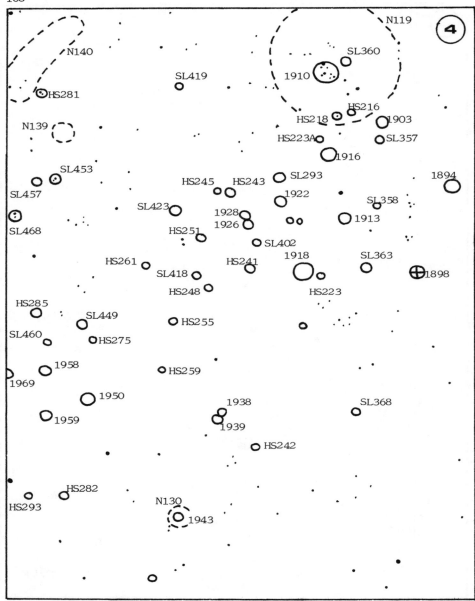

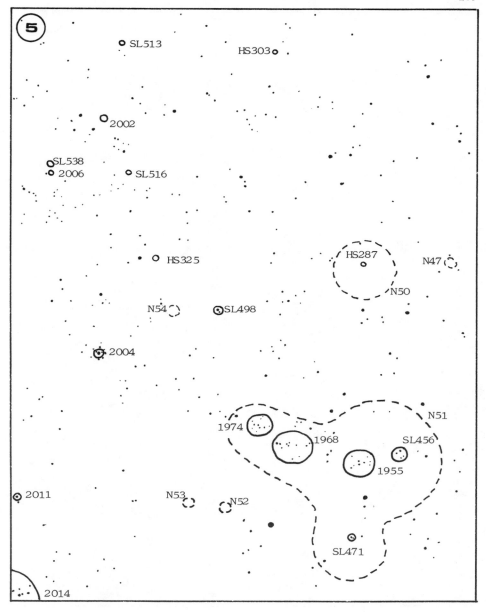

5

SL513

HS303

2002

SL538
2006

SL516

HS325

HS287

N47

N50

N54

SL498

2004

1974

1968

N51

SL456

1955

2011

N53

N52

SL471

2014

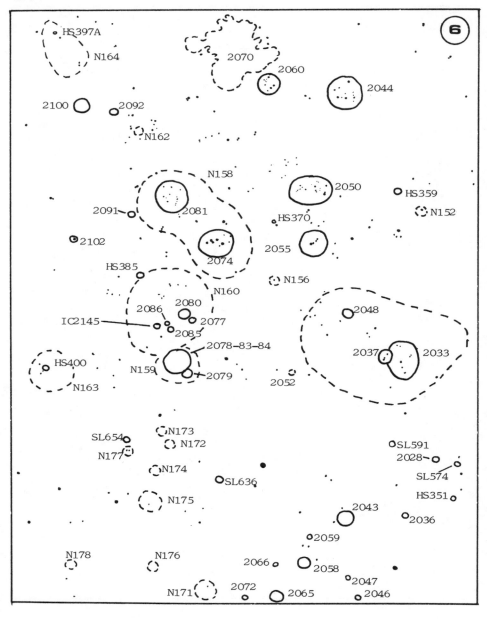

Appendices

APPENDIX 3: OBSERVING THE SMALL MAGELLANIC CLOUD.

The Small Magellanic Cloud (SMC), being that much smaller, more
distant and less rich than the LMC, does not present so impressive a
sight. Nevertheless, it does contain a number of objects of interest and
many of these are shown on the contour diagram in this Appendix. Since
it is unlikely that much beyond the 35 NGC objects in the SMC will be
found in most amateur instruments the objects identified are limited to
this catalogue, with the addition of a few IC objects.

The chart was prepared from examination of prints ESO(B)029 and
ESO(B)051 and reference to the RNGC. The symbols adopted are as
described in Appendix 2. It should be noted however, that there is still
some controversy over the classification of some objects; NGC 330, for
example, which is quite a bright object and one would imagine easily
classified, is variously described in the technical literature as either
a rich open cluster or a 'blue globular'. In this Appendix I have used
the globular classification, based on the suggestion of Janes and Carney
(IAU Symp. 85, 'Star Clusters', p. 349 - 352).

The North point and scale are shown on the diagram itself.

As a further aid to observers, some of the more prominent SMC objects
are listed below, together with their positions for Epoch 2000.0:

NGC	R.A.	Dec.	mag.	Type	Notes
121	00 26.8	−71 32	10.6	GCl.	
152	00 32.8	−73 09	12.0	GCl.	
220	00 40.5	−73 24	11.5	OCl.	
249	00 45.5	−73 05		Neb.	
292	00 52.7	−72 50		----	SMC centre
330	00 56.2	−72 29	9.6	GCl.	
339	00 57.7	−74 29	11.9	GCl.	
346	00 59.1	−72 11	10.3	Neb. OCl.	
361	01 02.2	−71 33	11.8	GCl.	
371	01 03.3	−72 05		Neb. OCl.	
416	01 08.1	−72 21	11.0	GCl.	
419	01 08.3	−72 53	10.0	GCl.	
456	01 14.4	−73 17		Neb. OCl.	First of chain of clusters

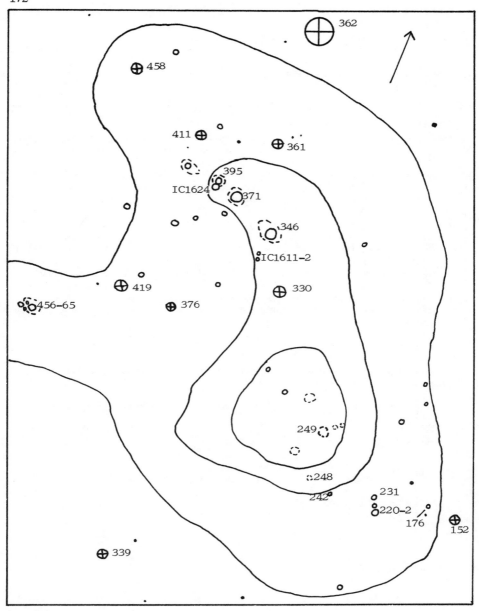

Appendices

APPENDIX 4: W.S.Q.J. ARTICLES RELATING TO SOUTHERN SKY OBJECTS.

Because of the number of objects covered in this volume, the descriptions are of necessity summaries. However, more detailed descriptions of many of the objects can be found in back issues of the Webb Society Quarterly Journal. The following is a record of these references, complete to July 1985, the articles being listed by author.

Further observations are also to be found in the miscellaneous reports of the Webb Society Observing Sections, which are also to be found in the Quarterly Journal.

....

David A. Allen

'Some Observations from Mt. Wilson', W.S.Q.J. Sept. 1971, p. 16 - NGC 1788 (60-inch), Merrill 2-1 (100-inch), Minkowski 2-9 (100-inch), Hubble 4 (100-inch).

'South African Interlude', W.S.Q.J. October 1973, p.10 - NGC 3699 (40-inch), NGC 6302 (40-inch).

'Australian Interlude: Part 3', W.S.Q.J. April 1980, p.15 - AP Librae (154-inch), NGC 5128 (154-inch), NGC 1097 (154-inch), NGC 2070 (154-inch), NGC 4650A (154-inch), NGC 5291 (154-inch), NGC 330 (154-inch), Roberts 22 (154-inch), IC 4329A (154-inch), η Carinae (154-inch).

'The Cluster', W.S.Q.J. July 1983, p. 16 - omega Centauri (40-inch).

David & Brenda Branchett

'Observing the Fornax Cluster of Galaxies', W.S.Q.J. April 1982, p.14 - NGC 1316, NGC 1317, NGC 1326, NGC 1341, NGC 1350, NGC 1351, NGC 1365, NGC 1374, NGC 1379, NGC 1380, NGC 1381, NGC 1382, NGC 1386, NGC 1387, NGC 1389, NGC 1399, NGC 1404, NGC 1427 & NGC 1437 (5-inch & 6-inch).

Ronald J. Buta

'Southern Celestial Objects: Part 2', W.S.Q.J. April 1983, p.1 - NGC 104 (36-inch), NGC 121 (40-inch), NGC 330 (40-inch), NGC 346 (40-inch), NGC 419 (40-inch), NGC 1313 (40-inch), NGC 1433 (158, 40 & 16-inch), NGC 1448

Appendices

(40-inch), NGC 1512 (36-inch), NGC 1566 (40 & 36-inch), NGC 2070 (36, 16 & 6-inch), NGC 3372 (16 & 6-inch), NGC 6101 (40-inch), NGC 6215 (40-inch), NGC 6221 (40-inch), NGC 6300 (158 & 40-inch), NGC 6302 (40-inch), NGC 6337 (40-inch), NGC 6362 (40-inch), NGC 6438 (40-inch), NGC 6744 (158 & 24-inch), NGC 6769-70-71 (40-inch), NGC 7204 (40-inch), NGC 7424 (40-inch), NGC 7496 (40-inch), NGC 7531 (158, 40 & 24-inch), NGC 7702 (158 & 36-inch), NGC 7713 (40-inch).

Jeffrey A. Corder

'A Southern Cluster of Galaxies', W.S.Q.J. July 1985, p. 7 - NGC 5291, NGC 5292, NGC 5298, NGC 5302, NGC 5304, IC 4329, MCG 05-33-005, 009, 011, 014, 015, 017, 019, 020, 024 & 2 anon. galaxies (12½-inch).

Colin Henshaw

'The Magellanic Clouds', W.S.Q.J. January 1985, p. 4 - observations of the LMC and SMC made with 12x40 binoculars.

Steven J. Hynes

'Observing in Sagittarius', W.S.Q.J. October 1974, p. 10 - NGC 6523-30, NGC 6611, NGC 6613, NGC 6618 & IC 4725 (8½-inch).

'Galactic Clusters in Scorpius', W.S.Q.J. April 1982, p. 8 - NGC 6231, NGC 6242, NGC 6322, NGC 6405, NGC 6475 & H.12 (4¼-inch RFT).

'The Visual Morphology of the Nebula NGC 6523', W.S.Q.J. October 1982, p. 6 - NGC 6523-30 (4¼-inch RFT).

'A Southern Asterism', W.S.Q.J. April 1983, p. 24 - asterism at R.A. 07h. 24m., Dec. -31° 50' (2000) CMa. (4¼-inch RFT).

'Galactic Clusters in Canis Major', W.S.Q.J. July 1984, p. 7 - NGC 2287 (8½-inch & 4¼-inch RFT), NGC 2362 (4¼-inch RFT).

'Galactic Clusters in Puppis', W.S.Q.J. October 1984, p. 3 - NGC 2422 (8½ inch), NGC 2437-8 (8½-inch), NGC 2439, NGC 2447, NGC 2451, NGC 2477 & NGC 2489 (4¼-inch RFT).

Ronald J. Morales

'The Sculptor Group of Galaxies', W.S.Q.J. October 1984, p. 7 - NGC 55 (8-inch), NGC 253 (8-inch) & NGC 300 (6-inch).

Appendices

Malcolm J. Thomson

'Observations of Some Interesting Objects South of the Celestial
Equator', W.S.Q.J. July 1977, p. 5 – NGC 253, NGC 2283, NGC 2292-3-5, NGC
2298, NGC 2467, NGC 2818-2818A, NGC 5128, NGC 5139 (16½-inch).

Appendices

APPENDIX 5: OBSERVATIONAL DATA RELATING TO THE STAR η CARINAE.

A brief description of η Carinae is given on page 20.   To enable
observers to monitor this remarkable star, this Appendix gives a chart
and sequence for the object, plus a light-curve of the activity of the
star from 1820 - 1952.   The material in this Appendix has been kindly
provided by Dr. Gerard de Vaucouleurs.

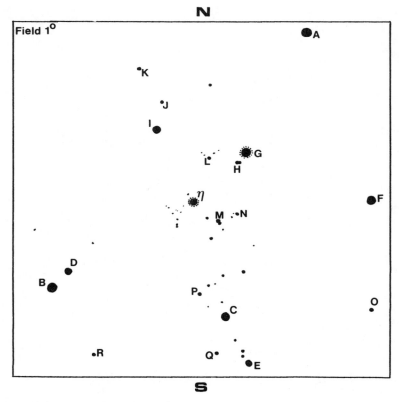

Chart by GdV, redrawn SJH (1986).

Appendices

Comparison Stars for η Carinae.

Star	HD	Spec.	m_V	Notes
A	92964	B3p	5.63	
B	93737	A2p	6.26	zero point of sequence.
C	93206	B0	Var.	QZ Car., EB, 6.2-6.5.
D	93695	B5	6.67	
E	93131	Ocp	6.71	
F	92740	Ocp	Var.	see Note 1.
G	93128-9	B+B	7.25::	in small group, fuzzy with low power.
H	93160-1	B+A3	7.65:	double, not resolved with low power.
I	93420	M2	Var.	BO Car., Lc, 7.2-8.5.
J	93403	B0	7.50	
K	93469	A5	8.12	
L	93250	B	7.80:	
M	93204-5	B+B	8.01:	double, not resolved with low power.
N	93162	Oc	8.33::	
O	92741	B3	7.78::	
P	93281	K0	8.03::	

Notes

1. Although this star is given as variable by the Cordoba observers in the Uranometria Argentina, it is not listed in the modern catalogues of recognized variables. It is, however, definitely variable, the observed visual magnitudes m_V ranging from about 6.9 to 6.55 with no obvious periodicity; the star deserves further study - GdV.

Accuracy of Sequence

The error in the zero point of the visual magnitudes (star B) is believed to be less than ±0.05; the p.e. of the magnitude differences measured from this zero point is about ±0.01, except where marked : or ::, when it is about ±0.02 or ±0.03 mag., respectively.

Appendices

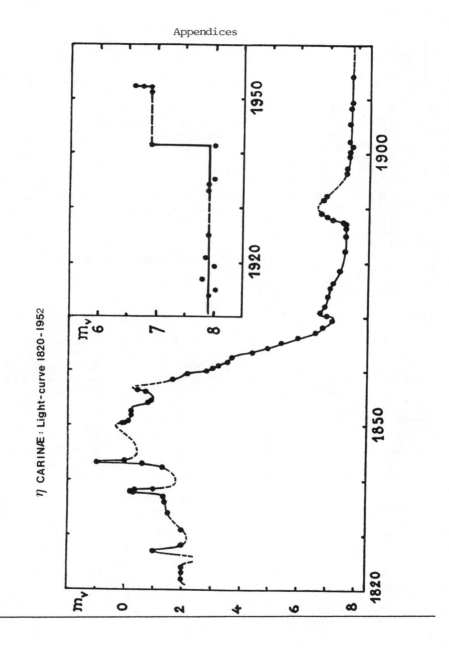

η CARINÆ : Light-curve 1820-1952

Appendices

APPENDIX 6: THE GUM NEBULA & RELATED FEATURES.

Stretching over a vast area of the southern Milky Way is a complex shell of nebulous filaments and diffuse patches called the Gum Nebula, named after Colin S. Gum, the Australian astronomer who discovered it in 1952 (ref. 1). The faintness of the nebulosity, together with its scale, some 30° in extent, was responsible for keeping it hidden from observers until such a comparatively recent time. A chart of the central region, showing some of the brightest features, is shown at figure 1, and more details regarding objects on the chart are given in Table 1. Most of the significant areas of the Gum Nebula are contained within the triangle of bright stars ζ Puppis, γ Velorum and λ Velorum. The chart is based on the composite photograph given in ref. 2.

The Vela SNR

One significant component of the Gum Nebula is a half-shell of filaments similar to the Veil Nebula in Cygnus, called Vela X (its designation given when first discovered by radio astronomers). This is believed to be the remnant of a massive supernova explosion which occurred about 11,800 years ago, and which lies at a distance of about 460 pc. It has been estimated that the SN may have been as bright as -10, seen from Earth. The fact that the remnant remains visible is largely due to the energy imparted to it by the Vela pulsar (PSR 0833-45). Interestingly, the pulsar does not lie at the centre of the optical remnant but about one degree to the west. Being comparatively young it has a rapid pulse period of 0.089 seconds; this is believed to be equal to its rotation rate. The pulsar is exceptionally faint so that, although discovered by radio astronomers in 1968, its optical counterpart was not identified until 1977. At magnitude 24, it is the faintest star to have had its brightness determined. The position of the Vela pulsar is shown by the + on the chart at figure 1.

Other Emission Nebulae

On the eastern side of the chart are several dashed areas which are discrete emission nebulae. The italic numbers indicate the identification of the objects in the 1960 catalogue of Rodgers, Campbell and Whiteoak (RCW), ref. [9]. These all lie at considerably greater distances than the SNR. The nearest is believed to be RCW 32 at 700 pc., and the most distant may be RCW 40. This is a compact HII region which, no stars having been identified as associated with it, has not had its distance determined optically, however, from radio observations, a radial velocity has been found which has been interpreted as indicating a distance of 2600 pc. (ref. 2). I have not come across any reports of these RCW objects having been observed visually, either by amateur or

Appendices

professionals. RCW 40 appears photographically dense and is about 8' in diameter so may be worth searching out.

Extensive regions of tenuous nebulosity are found around the binary γ Velorum (mag. 1.88, type WC8+O9) and ζ Puppis (mag. 2.25, type O5I) and these hot, massive stars, which lie at about 300 pc. and 360 pc. respectively, are believed to be responsible for the illumination of this interstellar haze, however, part could be due to the SNR.

Bok globules in the Gum Nebula

Bok globules are small, compact clouds, often quite regular, with sizes of typically 0.15 - 0.8 pc., masses between $15M_\odot$ and $60M_\odot$ and temperatures in the range 9° K - 16° K. Bok suggested that these globules might represent a stage in the formation of stars from the interstellar medium and, although star formation is now believed to occur largely in giant molecular clouds, there is certainly a significant body of evidence to indicate that some star formation is associated with the globules.

About 40 globules have been identified in the Gum Nebula. A number of these, because of their dense 'heads' and streaming, lower density 'tails' are called 'cometary globules'. They were first discovered by Hawarden and Brand (ref. 4) during an inspection of hypersensitized IIIaJ plates, taken for the ESO/SRC Southern Sky Survey with the 48-inch UKST. The first two seen are quite close together in the sky and parallel so that initially the phenomenon was suspected to be an unusual form of plate blemish. Hawarden and Brand reported 12 cometary globules in their original paper but more were soon found and Zealey et al. (ref. 5) list 36 in their paper. Almost all of these appear to be associated with the Gum Nebula and their tails point directly away from one of two distinct centres within that structure.

The morphology of the cometary globules could be attributed to one of several causes, in particular, the effects of a supernova explosion, intense stellar winds, ultraviolet radiation and the expansion of an HII region. However, it should be noted that the explosion which produced the Vela X SNR could not be responsible because, as a result of its youth, the effects would not have spread as far as some of the more distant globules or caused tails several parsecs long in the available time. The effects of a more ancient supernova however, can not be entirely excluded.

CG 1 and Bernes 135

Typical of the cometary globules is CG 1 which has a head 2' across and a tail 25' long (corresponding to actual sizes of 0.3 pc. and 3.2 pc., respectively). This feature, like others of its class, is extremely

Appendices

faint and is unlikely to be observed visually.   Indeed, the only visual
observation I have seen is one reported by David A. Allen and here the
3.9m. A.A.T. was used: "Cometary globules......have bright rims surrounding
a dark blob, and long bright tails. 'Bright' is, however, a relative term.
CG 1 is the brightest, but all I could see was the misty outline of its
head, and a luminous haze winding its way through a scattering of 16th
magnitude stars" (ref. 8).

Although CG 1 itself might not be visible in all but the largest
telescopes there is a star, close to the head of the globule, Bernes 135
(ref. 3), which could be observed with smaller instruments, being of about
magnitude 10.6. This star exhibits features typical of a pre-main sequence
object and appears to be variable by at least 0.8 mag., though this has not
been studied comprehensively. It has a spectrum which is clearly composite
with absorption and emission elements, and appears to be of type F1 - F2.
Henize (ref. 6) discovered its $H\alpha$ emission and listed it as He 3-32 in his
catalogue.

A more detailed account of this fascinating star can be found in
Reipurth (ref. 7). The following parameters are suggested:

Bernes 135.   R.A. 07h. 19.0m., Dec. -44° 35' (2000).

Luminosity	–	$45 - 50$ $L_{\odot}$
T_e	–	6800° K
Mass	–	$2.5 - 3.0$ $M_{\odot}$
Radius	–	5 $R_{\odot}$
Age	–	1 million years
Distance	–	450 pc.

The star is embedded on the southern edge of a small, comparatively
bright, 'reverse-S' shaped nebula, about 3' in its greatest extent, at the
apex of the head. This is part of the rim of the globule.

The GDC 1 - GDC 7 complex

This is a remarkable region of dark clouds and globules which, though
not of a cometary shape, are clearly associated with the Gum Nebula. Like
the cometary globules, most of them are sharply delineated and bordered by
narrow bright rims on the side facing the centre of the Gum Nebula.
Though of similar nature to the cometary globules, their form has led to
them being catalogued as Gum Dark Cloud (GDC) 1 - 7, instead of being
given CG numbers.

GDC 1 (= ESO 210-6A) is associated with the Herbig-Haro objects HH 46
and HH 47. Infrared searches at 2.2 μm. and 10 μm. have failed to reveal
evidence of any embedded star in the globule so, although a star as

Appendices

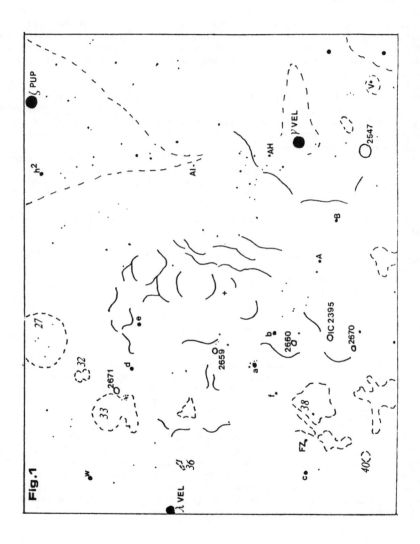

Appendices

Figure 1. Sketch chart of the central region of the Gum Nebula.

Notes: broken lines indicate the outline of the brighter nebulous areas
and those marked by 2-figure italic numbers are objects in the RCW
catalogue. The filamentary structure represents the brighter parts of
the Vela X SNR, the Vela pulsar being indicated by '+'. Open circles are
open clusters in the field.

....

Table 1. Data relating to objects shown on the chart at figure 1.

Object	R.A. (2000)	Dec.	Type	mag.	Notes
Open clusters					
NGC 2547	08 10.7	−49 16	II 2 p	4.7	
IC 2395	08 41.1	−48 12	II 3 p	4.6	
NGC 2660	08 42.2	−47 09	I 3 m	8.8	
NGC 2659	08 42.6	−44 57	III 3 m	8.6	Vel OB1
NGC 2670	08 45.5	−48 47	II 2 p	7.8	
NGC 2671	08 46.2	−41 53	I 3 p	11.6	
Variable Stars					
V Pup	07 58.2	−49 15	EB	4.7-5.2	
AH Vel	08 12.0	−46 39	Cepheid	5.5-5.9	
AI Vel	08 14.1	−44 34	Sct	6.4-7.4	
PSR 0833 −45	08 35.3	−45 11	Pulsar	24	
FZ Vel	08 58.9	−47 14	Sct	5.15-5.17	
Nebulae					
RCW 27	08 38.1	−40 20			= Gum 14
RCW 32	08 44.6	−41 17			= Gum 15
RCW 33	08 51.1	−42 02			= Gum 17
RCW 36	08 59.1	−43 41			= Gum 20
RCW 38	08 59.7	−47 27			= Gum 22-23-24
RCW 40	09 02.4	−48 42			= Gum 25

The data provided in this table is extracted from 'Sky Catalogue 2000.0 -
Volume 2', by A. Hirshfeld & R.W. Sinnott, Cambridge University Press,
1985, with the exception of the positions for RCW 27, 33 and 36.

Appendices

Figure 2. Chart of the cometary globule CG 1 and its relation to the star Bernes 135.

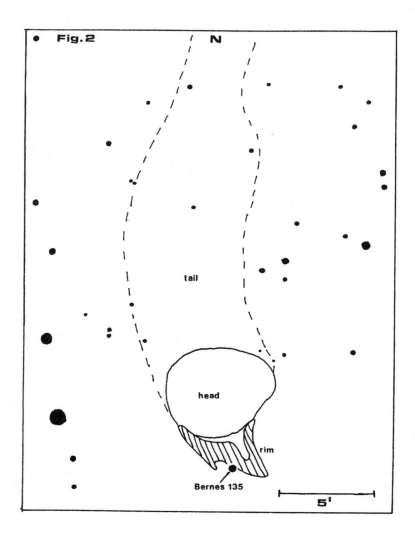

Appendices

continued from page 181.

luminous as Bernes 135 is precluded, a low-luminosity star could still be present (ref. 7).

This complex of dark nebulae is centred on about R.A. 08h. 25m., Dec. -50° 52' (2000) and all lie within a 25' radius of this point. The largest are about 5' in diameter.

Evolution of globules in the Gum Nebula

Reipurth (ref. 1) suggests that the cometary globules in the Gum Nebula are the precursors of the more well-known isolated Bok globules. They formed when the massive star ζ Puppis ignited in a region of small, clumpy molecular clouds. The intense UV radiation disrupted the clouds and separated out the less dense material, which formed a tail in the shadow of the more dense core. The continuing UV emission from ζ Puppis, of course, still affects the globules and causes them to evaporate, albeit slowly. A star as massive as ζ Puppis, however, is inevitably shortlived on the cosmic timescale and most of the globules will survive the disruptive effects of the UV bombardment, enabling stars to form within them. In cases where the globules have not evaporated or borne stars , it seems they will eventually dissipate.

Incidentally, the association of these objects with areas of star formation is confirmed by the fact that the young cluster NGC 5367 is embedded in the cometary globule CG 12.

Conclusion

Sadly, most of the interesting features of the Gum Nebula are well beyond the capabilities of most amateur equipment, requiring large aperture telescopes and/or long exposure photographs to resolve. Having said this it does appear that little, if any, attempt has been made by favourably placed, well equipped amateurs to search for objects in the Gum Nebula. It would be interesting to know, for example, whether any of the RCW objects or the GDC 1 - 7 dark nebulae, or the small nebula around Bernes 135 could be seen visually or photographically using amateur equipment; in this respect perhaps some of the new generation of nebular filters might be usefully employed. Also, the variability of such an interesting star as Bernes 135 could be monitored.

. . . .

References

1. Gum, C.S.; Observatory, _72_, 151, 1952.

Appendices

References (continued)

2. Miller, E.W. & Muzzio, J.C.; Sky & Telescope <u>49</u>, 94, 1975.

3. Bernes, C.; Astron. Astrophys. Suppl., <u>29</u>, 65, 1977.

4. Hawarden, T.G. & Brand, P.; M.N.R.A.S., <u>175</u>, 19P, 1976.

5. Zealey, W.J. (et al.); Astrophysical Letters, <u>23</u>, 119, 1983.

6. Henize, K.G.; Ap.J. Suppl., <u>30</u>, 491, 1976.

7. Reipurth, B.; E.S.O. Preprint No. 208, 1982.

8. Allen, D.A.; W.S.Q.J. No. 40, 17, 1980.

9. Rodgers, A.W., Campbell, C.T. & Whiteoak, J.B.; M.N.R.A.S. <u>121</u>, 103, 1960.

This Appendix is a revised version of an article, 'The Gum Nebula', by Steven J. Hynes, which was first published in W.S.Q.J. No. 62, October 1985.

Appendices

APPENDIX 7: CATALOGUE OF ADDITIONAL OBJECTS.

The following observations of southern deep-sky objects were received after the completion of the main catalogue section:

Open Clusters

NGC 2477: R.A. 07h 52.3m., Dec. -38° 33' (2000): Type I 2 r: Mag. 5.7: Diam. 25': Puppis.

12-inch: Lovely rich cluster with chains and festoons of stars. (Denis Dutton).
8-inch: Large and impressive. An almost round, compact group of about 50 stars. A small, more compact area noted in N. part of the cluster. (Ronald J. Morales).

NGC 2482: R.A. 07h 55.0., Dec. -24° 18' (2000): Type IV 1 m: Mag. 8.7: Diam. 18': Puppis.

8-inch: medium-sized cluster of about 20-25 stars, in a'starfish' shape. Stars of similar brightness. (Ronald J. Morales).
12x40 bin.: a small, faint cluster in a rich field. (Colin Henshaw).

NGC 2533: R.A. 08h 07.0m., Dec. -29° 54' (2000): Type III 1 p: Mag. 7.6: Diam. 3'.5: Puppis.

12-inch: very sparse cluster with a line of stars across it. (Denis Dutton)

NGC 2627: R.A. 08h 37.3m., Dec. -29° 57' (2000): Type III 2 m: Mag. 8.4: Diam. 11': Pyxis.

6-inch: a very faint, hazy cluster, only partly resolved even at x114. Elongated roughly N-S; about 10' at greatest extent. (Victor Hirsch).

IC 2391: R.A. 08h 44.1m., Dec. -53° 03' (2000): Type II 3 p: Mag. 2.6: Diam. 50': Vela.

12x40 bin.: a large, loose clustering, easily visible to the naked-eye and involving the star o Vel. Somewhat resembles the θ Carinae association. One bright double S.f. o Vel.itself. (Colin Henshaw).

Appendices

NGC 3105: R.A. 10h 00.8m., Dec. -54° 46' (2000): Type I 3 p: Mag. 9.7:
Diam. 2': Vela.

40-inch: 18 stars in a field 2' x 1'. (David A. Allen).

IC 2581: R.A. 10h 27.4m., Dec. -57° 38' (2000): Type I 3 m: Mag. 4.3:
Diam. 8': Carina.

40-inch: cluster of 30-40 stars in a field 4' - 5'; the brightest is of
about mag. 12 but a mag. 4 foreground star is also involved. (David A.
Allen).

Harvard 5: R.A. 12h 29.0m., Dec. -60° 46' (2000): Type II 3 p: Mag. 7.1:
Diam. 6': Crux.

20-inch: Faint cluster of 30 stars in a 6' field. (David A. Allen).
12-inch: Loose cluster of 20 or more bright stars. Rather sparse (Denis
Dutton).

NGC 4463: R.A. 12h 30.0m., Dec. -64° 48' (2000): Type I 3 p: Mag. 7.2:
Diam. 5': Musca.

40-inch: cluster of 20 stars in a 4' field, 2 of which are very bright.
(David A. Allen).

NGC 5316: R.A. 13h 53.9m., Dec. -61° 52' (2000): Type III 1 p: Mag. 6.0:
Diam. 14': Centaurus.

20-inch: loose cluster of about 70 stars in a 12' field. (David A. Allen).

NGC 6124: R.A. 16h 25.6m., Dec. -40° 41' (2000): Type II 3 m: Mag. 6.3:
Diam. 25': Scorpius.

12-inch: Large, loose cluster of bright stars. (Denis Dutton).
10-inch: At x59, fills about half the field. About 60 stars altogether.
(Ronald J. Morales).
6 -inch: Very pretty, concentrated cluster of possibly 80 - 100 stars of
about mag. 9 and below. Estimated diameter 32'. (Victor Hirsch).

NGC 6253: R.A. 16h 59.1m., Dec. -52° 43' (2000): Type I 3 m: Mag. 10.2:
Diam. 5': Ara.

12-inch: Wispy, web-like triangle of a few dozen faint stars. (Denis
Dutton).

Appendices

NGC 6451: R.A. 17h 50.7m., Dec. -30° 13' (2000): Type II 1 p: Mag. 8.2:
Diam. 8': Scorpius.

20-inch: faint but impressive cluster of about 70 stars in a 10' field.
(David A. Allen)

Globular Clusters

NGC 4372: R.A. 12h 25.8m., Dec. -72° 40' (2000): Type   : Mag. 7.8:
Con. cl. XII: Musca.

12-inch: large and well resolved, much more resembling an open than
globular cluster. A number of stars scattered across the field. (Denis
Dutton).

IC 4499: R.A. 15h 00.3m., Dec. -82° 13' (2000): Type   : Mag. 10.6:
Con. cl. XI: Apus.

12-inch: vague nebulosity without much condensation; not really
recognizable as a globular. Certainly not resolved. An apparent
foreground star lies dead centre. (Denis Dutton).

NGC 6453: R.A. 17h 51.4m., Dec. -34° 37' (2000): Type F : Mag. 9.9:
Con. cl. IV: Scorpius.

8-inch: small, round patch of light. Not resolved. (Ronald J. Morales).

Planetary Nebulae

IC 2448: R.A. 09h 07.1m., Dec. -69° 57' (2000): m(n) 11.5: m(s) 12.9:
Type IIb: Diam. 8": Carina.

12-inch: very small, perfectly round, featureless blue disc, very near to
β Carinae. (Denis Dutton).

IC 2501: R.A. 09h 38.8m., Dec. -60° 05' (2000): m(n) 11.3: m(s)   :
Type I : Diam. 25": Carina.

40-inch: uniform, circular, blue planetary of about mag. 11. Diameter 6".
(David A. Allen).

190

Appendices

IC 2553: R.A. 10h 09.3m., Dec. -62° 37' (2000): m(n) 13.0: m(s) 12.9:
Type : Diam. 9": Carina.

40-inch: oval nebula 6" x 4"in P.A. $30^\circ - 21^\circ$. Blue. Almost uniform;
soft outline. (David A. Allen).

Fg. 1 (PK 290+7°.1): R.A. 11h 28.6m., Dec. -52° 26' (2000): m(n) :
m(s) : Type III+VI: Diam. 25": Centaurus.

154-inch: symmetrical but unusually shaped. Elongated E-W, it is
elliptical with an axial ratio of 2:1. The nebula is almost uniformly
bright except for a dusky hourglass-shaped portion, N-S across the minor
axis. No central star seen. (David A. Allen).

IC 4191: R.A. 13h 08.8m., Dec. -67° 39' (2000): m(n) 12.0: m(s) :
Type II: Diam. 5": Musca.

40-inch: green, uniform, circular PN. No central star. (David A. Allen).
6 -inch: located with prism. Very faint; stellar at all powers. (Victor
Hirsch).

NGC 5189: R.A. 13h 33.5m., Dec. -65° 59' (2000): m(n) 10.3: m(s) 14.0:
Type V: Diam. 153": Musca.

6 -inch: easily seen at x32. At x230 it appears diamond-shaped, about
200"in greatest elongation. A bright star lies to the S. and a row of
small stars arch from the nebula to the S.W. (Victor Hirsch).

NGC 5315: R.A. 13h 53.9m., Dec. -66° 31' (2000): m(n) 13.0: m(s) 11.3:
Type II: Diam. 5": Circinus.

6 -inch: located and identified with a prism. Stellar at all powers, with
suspicion of a tiny disc at x230. (Victor Hirsch).

NGC 5873: R.A. 15h. 12.8m., Dec. -38° 08' (2000): m(n) 13.3: m(s) 13.6:
Type II: Diam. 3": Lupus.

40-inch: uniform, bright, sharp-edged PN, about 7" x 5". No central star
but faint star N.f. P.A. $100^\circ - 280^\circ$. Green in colour. (David A. Allen).
24-inch: this tiny object, at a magnification of x500, appears to be a
ring-shaped planetary nebula. No central star seen. Ring not uniformly
bright. (Ronald J. Buta).

Appendices

He 2-131: R.A. 15h 37.2m., Dec. -71° 55' (2000): m(n)   : m(s) 10.5:
Type   : Diam. 5": Apus.

40-inch: mag. 11, soft, almost stellar object. Rich turquoise in colour.
(David A. Allen).

M 1-26 (= HD 316248): R.A. 17h 46.0m., Dec. -30° 12' (2000): m(n)   :
m(s) 12.1: Type II: Diam. 4": Scorpius.

74-inch: non-stellar, green nebula. (David A. Allen).

Diffuse Nebulae

NGC 5189: R.A. 13h 34.2m., Dec. -65° 59' (2000): Type E: Size 3' x 2':
Musca.

24-inch: a very fine object exhibiting a considerable amount of structure.
It is a large, irregular nebula that bears a striking resemblance to an
S-shaped barred spiral galaxy. The 'bar' is diffuse and splits on one
side; the 'arms' are patchy and quite extensive, and they arch sharply off
the ends of the bar. I have never seen a photograph of this object but I
assume that the catalogues are correct in describing it as a galactic
nebula: it looked more like a barred galaxy than some real galaxies I have
seen! The surface brightness in the brighter parts is quite high.
(Ronald J. Buta).

Note: this object is also catalogued as RCW 76 and Gum 47.

NGC 6164-5: R.A. 16h 34.4m., Dec. -48° 03' (2000): Type E: Size 8' x 4':
Norma.

12-inch: large oval shell around an 8th mag. star. Barely seen and only
with a nebular filter but exhibits a bright knot on S. side of shell.
(Denis Dutton).

Note: the star is HD 148937 and the nebula is also catalogued as RCW 107
and Gum 52.

Galaxies

NGC 406: R.A. 01h 07.4m., Dec. -69° 53' (2000): Type   : Mag. 12.4:
Size 3'.8 x 1'.5: Tucana.

12-inch: small, condensed object containing no detectable structure.
(Denis Dutton).

Appendices

NGC 1187: R.A. 03h 02.6m., Dec. -22° 52' (2000): Type SBbc(s)I-II:
Mag. 11.3: Size 5'.5 x 3'.7: Eridanus.

10-inch: very bright, very large patch, becoming gradually brighter towards
the centre. Irregularly round. Star p. galaxy. (Ronald J. Morales).

NGC 1232: R.A. 03h 09.7m., Dec. -20° 34' (2000): Type Sc(rs)I: Mag. 10.5:
Size 7'.0 x 5'.5: Eridanus.

6 -inch: large, bright, roundish object. Slightly brighter centre.
(Ronald J. Morales).

NGC 1332: R.A. 03h 26.3m., Dec. -21° 21' (2000): Type $SO_1(6)$: Mag. 10.4:
Size 3'.4 x 1'.0: Eridanus.

10-inch: very bright object, extended S.W.-N.E., with a much brighter
compact nucleus. Star seen within outer nebulosity on p. side of galaxy.
In same field as NGC 1325. (Ronald J. Morales).

NGC 1401: R.A. 03h 39.4m., Dec. -22° 43' (2000): Type Sb: Mag. 12.5:
Size 2'.8 x 0'.7: Eridanus.

10-inch: found between NGC 1395 and NGC 1415, this object appears
irregularly round. Some mottling suspected with a.v. or, more specifically
there seems to be a dark lane along the centre of the galaxy but not
entirely cutting it in half. (Ronald J. Morales).

NGC 1439: R.A. 03h 44.8m., Dec. -21° 55' (2000): Type E1: Mag. 12.9:
Size 1'.0 x 0'.9: Eridanus.

10-inch: smallest of the group of galaxies which also includes NGC 1395,
NGC 1415 and NGC 1426. It is round with a slightly brighter core.
(Ronald J. Morales).

NGC 2090: R.A. 05h 47.0m., Dec. -34° 13' (2000): Type Sc(s)II: Mag. 12.4:
Size 2'.5 x 1'.0: Columba.

8 -inch: small, round, with a brighter centre. A.v. shows envelope to be
somewhat extended. (Ronald J. Morales).

Appendices

NGC 2179: R.A. 06h 08.0m., Dec. -21° 44' (2000): Type Sa: Mag. 13.0: Size 0'.9 x 0'.7: Lepus.

10-inch: small, faint, extended patch of light with a gradually brighter core. Faint star on N. tip and fainter star on S. tip. (Ronald J. Morales).

NGC 2207: R.A. 06h 16.5m., Dec. -21° 22' (2000): Type Sc(s)I.2: Mag. 11.4: Size 2'.8 x 1'.9: Canis Major.

10-inch: bright and large and seemingly of granular texture. Brighter core, offset towards p. edge. A.v. shows a slightly brighter area in f. edge, almost as if the galaxy has 2 cores. (Ronald J. Morales).

NGC 3256: R.A. 10h 27.8m., Dec. -43° 54' (2000): Type   : Mag. 11.3: Size 3'.5 x 2'.0: Vela.

40-inch: irregular nebulous patch, 40" x 60", with bright, almost circular, central region and fainter lobes in P.A. 90° and 250°. (David A. Allen).

NGC 4105/6: R.A. 12h 06.7m., Dec. -29° 46' (2000): Type SO1/2(3) & SB0/a (tides): Mag. 12.0 & 12.5: Size 1'.5 x 1'.5 & 1'.0 x 0'.8: Hydra.

10-inch: two galaxies seen close together but not touching. NGC 4105 is the brighter and has a brighter core. NGC 4106 is about the same size and shape as NGC 4105 but is less well-defined. (Ronald J. Morales).

NGC 5082-90-91: R.A. 13h 21.1m., Dec. -43° 44' (2000)*: Type E+E2+S: Mag.   : Size N/K (5082), 2'.6 x 2'.5 (5090), 2'.2 x 0'.4 (5091): Centaurus.

24-inch: the three objects are visible in nearly the same field of view. NGC 5090 and 5091 form a very beautiful and conspicuous pair. The brighter component, NGC 5090, appears slightly elongated and and diffuse while the fainter NGC 5091, a spiral, is nearly edge-on and shows a faint nucleus. The two are practically in contact. A fainter galaxy, NGC 5082, appears to the west and is round, diffuse and has a faint nucleus. (Ronald J. Buta).

* R.A. & Dec. identify the position of NGC 5090.

Appendices

NGC 5643: R.A. 14h 32.7m., Dec. -44° 10' (2000): Type S(B)cIII: Mag. 10.7:
Size 4'.6 x 4'.1: Lupus.

12-inch: large, low surface brightness object. Slightly oval. Exhibits
no other detail. (Denis Dutton).

NGC 7020: R.A. 21h 11.4m., Dec. -64° 03' (2000): Type SO: Mag. 12.4:
Size 4'.3 x 2'.3: Pavo.

154-inch: observed on the acquisition T.V. attached to the A.A.T. CCD
camera. NGC 7020 is an extended galaxy with two zones of surface
brightness: a bright inner ring and bulge followed by a 'gap', beyond
which there occurs a faint outer ring. What makes the inner regions
interesting is the hexagonal shape of the inner ring. It appears to be
composed of two spiral arcs which emerge from a box-shaped zone in the
centre of which is a small round core. The hexagonal shape changes
abruptly once the 'gap' is reached and then does not appear again because
the outer ring is a perfect ellipse. I think the inner regions would have
been visible had it been possible to observe with an eyepiece at prime
focus, where the CCD camera is installed. (Ronald J. Buta).

NGC 7552: R.A. 23h 16.2m., Dec. -42° 35' (2000): Type SBb: Mag. 10.7:
Size 3'.5 x 2'.5: Grus.

30-inch: very bright galaxy appearing as an extended glow crossed by a
weak enhancement, apparently a bar, but no spiral arms visible. Has a very
bright central nucleus. (Ronald J. Buta).

NGC 7764: R.A. 23h 50.9m., Dec. -40° 44' (2000): Type Ir: Mag. 12.3:
Size 1'.5 x 1'.0: Phoenix.

30-inch: an asymmetric glow in which is immersed a bar-shape.
(Ronald J. Buta).

Bibliography

Historical

Aitken, R.G.   'The Binary Stars'; Dover Publ. Inc., 1964.

Argyle, R.W.   'Webb Society Deep-Sky Observer's Handbook, Volume 1:
(ed. K. Glyn Jones)   Double Stars', second edition; Enslow, 1986.

Argyle, R.W.   'An Ambition Realised'; W.S.Q.J. No. 52, April 1983,
                        p. 21-23.

Ball, R.S.   'The Story of the Heavens'; Cassell & Co., 1905.

Buttman, G.   'Shadow of the Telescope'; C. Scribner, 1970.

Glyn Jones, K.   'The Search for the Nebulae'; Alpha Academic Press,
                        1975.

Herschel, J.   'Results of Astronomical Observations made during the
                        Years 1834 - 38 at the Cape of Good Hope'; Smith,
                        Elder & Co., 1847.

Lacaille, N.L.   Mem. Roy. Ac. Paris, 1755.

Lausten, S.   ' 'First Light' for the E.S.O. 3.6m. Telescope'; Sky &
                        Telescope, Vol. 53, No. 2, Feb. 1977, p. 97-103.

Shapley, H.   'Galaxies'; Harvard Univ. Press, 1972.
(rev. P. Hodge)

Stephen, S. &   'The Dictionary of National Biography'; Oxford Univ.
Lee, S.   Press, 1917.

Stone, R.   'Lick Observatory's Chile Station'; Sky & Telescope,
                        Vol. 63, No. 5, May 1982, p. 446-448.

Whitney, C.A.   'The Discovery of Our Galaxy'; Angus & Robertson, 1971.

                        'Report of the Anglo-Australian Telescope Board';
                        Australian Gov't Publ. Service, (miscellaneous issues).

Bibliography

Observational

Barker, E.S. &   'Webb Society Deep-Sky Observer's Handbook, Volume 2:
Allen, D.A.   Planetary & Gaseous Nebulae'; Enslow, 1979.
(ed. K. Glyn Jones)

Barker, E.S.   'Webb Society Deep-Sky Observer's Handbook, Volume 3:
(ed. K. Glyn Jones)   Open & Globular Clusters'; Enslow, 1980.

Barker, E.S.   'Webb Society Deep-Sky Observer's Handbook, Volume 4:
(ed. K. Glyn Jones)   Galaxies'; Enslow, 1981.

Burnham, R   'Burnham's Celestial Objects, Volume 1 - 3'; Dover
                         Publ. Inc., 1978.

Hartung, E.J.   'Astronomical Objects for Southern Telescopes';
                         Cambridge Univ. Press, 1984.

Technical

Athanassoula, E.   'Internal Kinematics and Dynamics of Galaxies'; IAU
(ed.)   Symp. 100, D. Reidel, 1983.

Foy, R.   'Chemical Composition in the Small Magellanic Cloud';
                         The Messenger (E.S.O.) No. 31, March 1983, p. 24.

Hesser, J.E. (ed.)   'Star Clusters'; IAU Symp. 85, D. Reidel, 1980.

Mc Robert, A.   'The Supermassive Star Debate'; Sky & Telescope,
                         February 1984, p. 134.

Melnick, J.   'R 136: the Core of the Ionizing Cluster of 30
                         Doradus'; The Messenger (E.S.O.) No. 32, June 1983,
                         p. 11.

Panagia, N.   'Infrared Observations of R 136, the Central Object of
(et al.)   the 30 Doradus Nebula'; Astrophysical Journal, 1983
                         July 15.

Pottasch, S.B.   'Planetary Nebulae'; D. Reidel, 1984.

Robinson, L.J.   'Galactic Cannabalism'; Sky & Telescope, February
                         1981, p. 108.

Bibliography

Technical (cont'd)

Solomon, P. &
Edmunds, M.G.
(ed.)
'Giant Molecular Clouds in the Galaxy'; Pergamon Press, 1980.

Atlases, Catalogues and Lists

Becvar, A.   'Atlas of the Heavens - II. Catalogue 1950.0'; Czech. Ac. Sci. & Sky Publishing Inc., 1964.

Collinder, P.   'Galactic Clusters'; Lund Ann. 2, 1931. (Cr.)

Dreyer, J.L.E.   'New General Catalogue of Nebulae and Clusters of Stars'; R.A.S., London, 1888. (NGC).

'Index Catalogue I'; R.A.S., London, 1895. (IC)

'Index Catalogue II'; R.A.S., London, 1908. (IC)

Evans, D.S. &
Thackeray, A.D.   'A Photographic Survey of Bright Southern Planetary Nebulae'; M.N.R.A.S. No. 5, 1950.

Hodge, P.W. &
Sexton, J.A.   '457 New Star Clusters of the Large Magellanic Cloud'; Astron. J. 71, 363, 1966. (HS)

Hodge, P.W. &
Wright, F.   'The Large Magellanic Cloud'; Smithsonian Inst., 1967.

Lyngå, G.   'Catalogue of Open Cluster Data'; Lund Observatory, 1981 (rev. 1983).

Minkowski, R.   'New Emission Nebulae'; P.A.S.P. 58, 305, 1946. (M X-XX)

Perek, L. &
Kohoutek, L.   'Catalogue of Galactic Planetary Nebulae'; Czech. Ac. Sci., 1967. (PK)

Sandage, A. &
Tamman, G.   'A Revised Shapley-Ames Catalogue of Bright Galaxies'; Carnegie Inst. of Washington, 1981. (RSA)

Shapley, H.   'Star Clusters'; Harvard Obs. Monograph No. 2, 1930. (H)

Bibliography

Atlases, Catalogues and Lists (cont'd)

Shapley, H. &
Lindsay, E.M.
'A Catalogue of Clusters in the Large Magellanic Cloud'; Irish Astron. Journal, 6, 74, 1963. (SL)

Sulentic, J.W. &
Tifft, W.G.
'Revised New General Catalogue of Nonstellar Astronomical Objects'; Univ. of Arizona Press, 1973. (RNGC)

Tirion, W.
'Sky Atlas 2000.0'; Sky Publ. Co. & Cambridge Univ. Press, 1981.

Trumpler, R.J.
'Open Star Clusters'; Lick Observatory Bulletin No. 420, 1930. (Tr.)

Vehrenberg, H.
'Atlas of Deep-Sky Splendors'; Cambridge Univ. Press, 1983.

Others

Ferris, T.
'Galaxies'; Stewart, Tabori & Chang (N.Y.), 1982.

Malin, D. &
Murdin, P.
'Colours of the Stars'; Cambridge Univ. Press, 1984.

Murdin, P. &
Allen, D.A.
'Catalogue of the Universe'; Cambridge Univ. Press, 1979.